AF415223

PRAISE FOR *YOU BELONG*

To: Anne Kramer
From: Sarah Schmitt
Subject: *You Belong*

Anne,

I am so thankful that you gave me the opportunity to read through your manuscript.

I LOVED IT! Let me start with that I *love* the blue sticker… those who have been around the milspouse life will understand the joy and horror that comes with a little piece of tape. I felt like you were writing about me and directly to me; you were writing about so many women, mothers, sisters, friends, and milspouses that I have worked with over the years, and you were describing it in such an intimate way that it could be any of us. I appreciated that your writing was friendly and kind, yet reflective and interactive, and that the reflection segments called us into action and brought us closer in. I did use them to take the time to reflect, especially about my mil framily.

I wanted to be shocked at some of your experiences, especially with the military in the sandbox and story about a few females, but as heartbreaking as they were, I couldn't truly be shocked—only saddened that such mindsets continue to prevail and everyone acts so shocked that it could still be happening. I think that any industry that has been predominately male-led or male-centric hasn't grown enough, either. (From personal experience, I still deal with it even amongst the Salvation Army and Disaster Response environments ALL the time.)

I think that this also carries over to your writing about being a military spouse and that same continued fight for identity. You brought so many relatable aspects to your writing that I was comforted in a way—like when a friend has read your diary entries or is privy to your deep thoughts that you think no one else understands. From the perspective of someone who has suffered with mental health for years, I thought more of my issues were just in my head, and your story tells me otherwise.

Thank you for sharing with me and giving me the time to reflect with you through your writing, for making me feel—not only as a friend, but as a reader—assured that I am not alone,. Your stories give breath and assurance to others who have had similar plights.

Your writing was beautiful and something to be emulated, and I hope you do write more.

Thank you again for allowing me to read and be a part of the process, *your* process—this manuscript that will so impact those who read it.

Sincerely, your friend and kindred spirit,
Sarah

PRAISE FOR *YOU BELONG*

"With transition being so hard for the military family, this read will motivate Dependents through those hard times."

— Raymond Black, III
CEO, Heavenly Counsel

"Anne sheds light on the resilience, strength, and sacrifices of military spouses and captures the essence of their experience, creating a narrative that resonates deeply with the reader. This book is not just a testament to those challenges and a powerful tool for navigating their unique and often unseen struggles, but a celebration of the unwavering spirit that defines the military spouse community. She reminds us that our uniqueness is not just a feature, but a source of strength. *You Belong* is a beautifully crafted exploration of identity, belonging, and the inherent beauty in embracing who we truly are.

— Crystal Bettenhausen-Bubulka, LCSW, MSG
Doctoral Student & Military Spouse

"Anne's life journey has made her the exceptional champion and guide for others in search of belonging."

— Brian Moore
COL(R), U.S. Army

YOU BELONG

A GUIDEBOOK FOR THE CAREER-MINDED WOMAN ON THE MOVE

RUTH ANNE KRAMER, LCSW

YOU BELONG

A Guidebook for the Career-Minded Woman on the Move

First Edition

Published by Tactical 16 Publishing
Colorado Springs, CO
www.Tactical16.com

ISBN: 978-1-943226-90-0 (paperback)
ISBN: 978-1-943226-89-4 (hardcover)

TABLE OF CONTENTS

Foreword..v

Preface...vii

Note From the Author About the Cover..............................ix

Introduction..1

PART I: THE PRICE OF SERVICE 3

    1. No Longer in Uniform..5

    2. Transitioning Into Civilian Life 7

    3. More Than A Pretty Face...9

PART 2: THE ESSENCE OF A MILITARY SPOUSE..............13

    4. Wizardess 15

    5. Imposter Syndrome..19

    6. You Are Sharing You 23

    7. Love-Hate Relationship 25

    8. The Art of Making Friends......................................27

    9. You Can Learn A Lot from an Interview........................31

    10. The Questions No One Talks About............................35

    11. Taking the Reins..39

    12. Your Voice Matters..41

PART 3: INGREDIENTS IN COURAGE..........................45

    13. Forgiveness 47

    14. Values..49

    15. Expectations...51

    16. Sacrifice 55

    17. Standards 57

**PART 4: IN A HELPING PROFESSION —
THE INTANGIBLE BLESSINGS IN OUR WORK**................59

    18. Magic Dust..61

    19. What If I Don't Know Everything 65

    20. You Are Not for Everyone 67

    21. Make Sure They Hear You Roar 69

    22. Grieving Process 73

    23. W.W.A.D. (What Would Anne Do) 77

PART 5: AS A MOTHER..**79**

    24. Motherhood and A Career................................81

    25. Honor Thy Children 85

    26. It Is the Little Things 89

PART 6: UNCOVERED LESSONS....................**93**

    27. Don't Take the First "No" as the Final Answer.....................95

    28. Power 99

    29. Scapegoats & Shame..............................101

    30. My Invalid Fear....................................103

    31. Disappointment...................................107

    32. Know Your Worth.................................111

    33. The Day I Fired A Friend.......................115

PART 7: NUTRIENTS FOR THE SOUL **119**

    34. Self-Care..121

    35. Learn to Heal 125

    36. Keep An "I Love Me" Box 127

    37. Boundaries...129

PART 8: TRAITS OF A DOYENNE **131**

    38. The Sweeper 133

    39. Be With Your People 135

    40. Know Your People.................................139

PART 9: THE LIONESS WOMAN.....................**143**

    41. Being Your Own Boss 145

    42. Be A Superwoman and Own It................149

    43. New Beginnings 151

    44. Make Your Own Timeline 153

    45. Giving Back 155

Conclusion: Be A Changemaker.................................159

Acknowledgments 163

About the Author

About the Publisher

To my two spitfire daughters, Amelia and Julianne.
You can be anything you want, and you belong in any place you are.

FOREWORD

The first time I met Anne, she was introduced to me as the new Clinical Director (Boss Lady) for a non-profit agency we both briefly worked at while living in Hawaii. If you keep reading, she speaks about the professional trauma we both experienced while working for this agency. Keeping that professional work relationship was challenging because we had so much in common. We were both professional women and military wives. If you know anything about that lifestyle, meeting another military wife who does put her career to the forefront just like her husband, is a rare find. In my experience, meeting other military wives consists of getting coffee together on a Monday and having remedial conversations. The moment I met Anne, I knew we would get along well. Now, she is my sister in military life, motherhood, womanhood, and friendship. I can genuinely say she will be a part of my "tribe" forever.

This dynamic guide of "Tricks of the Trade" covers it all. From professionalism-wise, being okay with not knowing everything in your career, to putting your job first, and my favorite topic, "The Essence of a Military Spouse," which has more diamonds than the bracelet you always wanted. My sister does what she does best, explaining the common ground. What I mean by this is that she has an act of being relatable in all situations. She will probably kill me for saying this, but Anne can have you tell her your life story and give you feedback professionally. Then she can also go out all night and hit the dance floor like the best of them. This book leads with how truly down-to-earth she is. That's what makes her a great social worker and therapist. She inspires you to do better and be better, all while staying true to yourself.

— New Age Feminist *Troshaunda Elie*

PREFACE

"*You are not from here.*" That was the explanation I was given for not being offered any of the three management positions I had applied for and for which I knew I was qualified. To make matters worse, the "You are not from here" rationale was also used to offer me, instead, a non-managerial position for which I was ridiculously overqualified. Since when, I wondered, was colloquialism or residency status a requirement for employment? Unfortunately, this was not the first time I had been treated like an alien when my transitory lifestyle took me to unfamiliar areas of the country. In fact, it has happened to me so often, and in so many different situations, that it has become the impetus for writing this book.

For all the people who have ever been the new kid in class, the pledge in the social club, the new family in the neighborhood, the trainee on the job, the visitor in the congregation, or the new parent in the PTA, this book is for you. For all people who have ever hit a glass ceiling, been stymied by the status quo, mystified by jargon, or thwarted by standard operating procedures, this book is for you. For all the people whose identity has been defined by your spouse, your children, your heritage, your body, your clothes, or your accent, this book is for you.

Because I am a woman, I am writing this from a woman's point of view. I realize that military spouses can be men and women in different combinations. I know that men can organize play dates for their children, and serve in civic, social, educational, religious, recreational, and support groups the same as women.

I understand that men are productive colleagues of mine in the fields of social services and helping professions. I've learned that men can be mentors, confidants, leaders, team members, and cheerleaders. I've also learned that men can be petty, conniving, back-biting, and even bitchy. So, although I am writing with a woman's voice from a woman's perspective, the lessons I've learned can be applied to anyone on the move, man, or woman.

The purpose of this book is to provide lessons learned and words of encouragement in hopes of helping you to overcome any anxiety, doubt, or fear you have of pursuing a career as a military spouse, veteran, or woman in general. This quest you are embarking on is a calling and a blessing in one. Even if you find days that you question, "Is this for me?" That's okay, it either is or is not. Those are the days that push you out of your comfort zone and force you to grow. Find the lesson and embrace it. The key realization you must learn to embody, always, is that only you can decide whether you belong. No one can make that decision for you.

Now, let's get moving. Together.

NOTE FROM THE AUTHOR ABOUT THE COVER

This guidebook for "the woman on the move" has been created for women who have or are planning to relocate geographically, and for women who are advancing (or who desire to advance) in their careers.

If you are not familiar with the image used on the cover, it is an inventory sticker used in military PCS (permanent change of station) moves to identify belongings. The stickers have a lot number (which represents you/your family) as well as an item number, and they are used with the intention of keeping your possessions together as you move.

The blue moving sticker on the cover with the number 000 represents the start of a significant move in your life; a new beginning, the place where you will stake your claim and build your future like the courageous pioneer you are. It also defines the physical space you are occupying at this very moment.

Whether or not you arrived here by choice and regardless of what anyone else says or does, *you belong*.

YOU BELONG

INTRODUCTION

I want to take you on a voyage of discovery as you read through this book. Although there will not be a specific destination, there is the hope of arriving at a state of being, of complete self-acceptance. I desire to instill in you the courage to show up completely without hesitancy, without a desire to run and hide, change, or shrink any piece of who you are. I know there will be moments when you will be questioned and challenged by others and even grapple with self-doubt. I have been there and continued to face those demons at times. Those demons have then turned into gifts, which I have incorporated into nine different sections in this book that touch on aspects of roles you may hold, character traits, lessons learned, career hurdles, ways to take care of yourself, leadership advice, and on being a boss.

While reading, I encourage you to keep an open mind. I have included reflections to consider at the end of each section to push you closer to relating to others and finding your true self. This tool for introspection is valuable beyond measure. We each have our own unique journey, but we can all relate to the pain and joy experienced in our individual journeys.

I strongly believe this book is a vital resource due to the lack of discussion today about the challenges faced by women in the workforce. There are countless deficits in conversations about the obstacles women come up against while serving in uniform, being military spouses, transitory workers at all levels, and by women who are the born and raised "locals" of their town. This leads to a disconnect between each of these subgroups. By creating a space for dialogue about these heavy, draining, thorny, and, at times debilitating hurdles, we make room for professional and personal development. The new insight gained through having these much-needed heart-to-hearts will birth compassion and understanding, as well as make room for self-acceptance.

I remember going to an employment class in 2014 on Fort Bliss in El Paso, Texas, at the start of my social work career, with hopes for all the answers to be given to me. Unfortunately, that did not happen; honestly, I realize now, no one has all the answers. I was given examples of how to write a fancy resume and taught how to find all the "important" websites to post my resume. But what was extremely unfortunate was that no one told me it would be hard. They said, "You'll have to apply to many jobs to increase your chances of getting hired," but they did not have a real honest conversation about the pain I might endure during the process.

I'm here to tell you just that, it will be hard and at times overwhelming, but my friend, it will be worth it. You will endure roadblocks and heartache but don't lose sight of why you started this journey and where you want to be at the end of it. I've compiled all my blood, sweat, and tears into this book and tied it nicely with a bow. This is proof that even if our experiences are not beautiful or shiny, the wisdom gleaned on the other side is truly a gift.

PART ONE

THE PRICE OF SERVICE

All right, this part of my gift to you touches on the aspect of *service*. Service can apply to those who have served in the military, the police force or sheriff departments, or as firefighters or other first responders. You do not have to have served nor know someone who has worn a uniform to understand the intricacies of service. Again, we all know pain and joy, and what it means to sacrifice. Sacrifice for someone in uniform could mean missing the birth of a child, missing a child's first milestone, not being able to attend a friend's wedding, or even going to the funeral of a loved one. These are events that are missed because service to one's country was expected of the service member.

For those reading this that do not have that direct experience with the military journey, I will use some military jargon throughout this section, such as *commander*, which translates to boss or manager, and *unit*, meaning place of employment or company. Put yourself in a service member's shoes while reading and you'll gain a better understanding of what it means to serve. The lessons uncovered can be applied across many career fields.

Reflections: Please use these reflection sections to better understand who you are, why things are the way they are, and where you'd like to see yourself moving closer to in your personal and professional life. I want you to gain an understanding of what truly lights the fire in your soul.

Regarding sacrifice, for example, I put my ability to pursue higher education on hold by serving in the military. I knew that I wanted to work in the mental health field but through my service that sacrifice pushed me closer to the exact area in the mental health field that felt right for me, as a social worker. I probably would not be working with veterans and their families in my career had I not worn the uniform myself. I can either see this as an impediment or a gift because it led me to where I find myself today. Standing up for women, educating others on injustice when it shows up, and being an example for my children ignite the fire deep within me.

Then, concerning a time when someone sacrificed for me, was when my husband took an overseas assignment while in the military for one year for me and our kids. By him taking that assignment, I was afforded the ability to work in my private therapy practice longer. This kept our kids stabilized in a familiar environment instead of having to move again and risk my husband likely deploying and leaving us in an unfamiliar environment once again. Thus, my husband missed out on a great deal of witnessing our children grow at the young ages of six months, eighteen months, and three years old. This was a priceless sacrifice for which I am forever grateful.

1. Can you remember a time you sacrificed something (a thing/event) for someone else? What was that? What is the lesson gained from that sacrifice?

2. Can you remember a time when someone sacrificed for you? How was that for you to have experienced that? How have you shown gratitude to that person who sacrificed for you? If you have not shown gratitude, how can you now?

I

NO LONGER IN UNIFORM

"Each day you are leading by example. Whether you realize it or not or whether it's positive or negative, you are influencing those around you."

— Rob Liano

I served in the Army from 2004 to 2013. That time went fast and now, looking back on it, it was a blur. I learned a lot about what it is to be a woman in uniform, and I learned from individual women whom I admired and who served alongside me daily. Female soldiers would come to me and say things like, "You are the only female commander I ever had," and, "You really make a difference, thank you for all you do." I had male soldiers say to me, "Thanks for believing in me." I also learned a lot about myself through coworkers who did not support me and stood against me.

That opposition, I later realized, became a form of workplace trauma which I will discuss in greater detail in subsequent sections. I learned that I knew the difference between right and wrong and that I needed to stand my ground to gain respect. I also realized that I teach other people how to treat me through what I do and don't allow. I did not learn most of these lessons within the moment I experienced them. I've been able to reflect on both the heartwarming experiences and teeth-gritting situations and have been able to still learn from those past experiences.

While in uniform, I was not aware at the time of how much it meant to those female soldiers to have a female commander. I also didn't realize that to those male soldiers, it did not matter I was a woman, it mattered that I did my job. I remember a time during a morning unit run when a young male soldier said to me, "I didn't fall out of the run because you didn't." You never know how much of an impact you have on those who surround you. Remember, you could be making a difference and not even know. Even though you may have once worn the uniform or perhaps you have never worn a uniform, you can always make a difference.

Reflection: This reflection space for you is based on the influence we have on others and that others have on us. I have shared examples with you about when it was brought to my attention afterward how I had affected my soldiers but did not know until they told me. Many people have come into my life that provided a much-needed influence that I am more consciously aware of now than I was then. I went to South Korea for my first duty station in the military at twenty-two years old. I was young, naïve, and far away from friends and family. There were male and female leaders that I served with who not only helped me to learn my job but also filled in the voids of mother and father figures. Their presence influenced me immensely, more than they knew. The same goes for leaders that affected me in negative ways. I had leaders in the military who berated me due to their own personal shortcomings when they could have supported and mentored me. This type of cruel influence created sparks of fire within me, which was anger at the time but today serves as logs on my fire to be the best leader I can be.

1. Who might you be influencing right now in your life, and in what ways?

____

____

____

____

____

2. Is there someone who influenced you without even knowing? If you could express gratitude to them today, what would you say?

____

____

____

____

____

2

TRANSITIONING INTO CIVILIAN LIFE

"Some people live an entire lifetime and wonder if they have ever made a difference in the world. A veteran does not have that problem."

— Ronald Reagan

It was 2013 and I was no longer wearing the uniform. I found myself asking, *"Now what?"* No one prepared me for all the foreign emotions coming up all at once. No one told me I'd lose my confidence along with my uniform. It was as if my emotional compass was out of whack, spinning every which way but north. Whether you are a veteran or not, moving to a new location and starting a new career can feel like embarking to a foreign land. I recommend you allow your internal compass to guide you in the direction where your emotions feel right most of the time. I believe what made things extra difficult for me was that my life not only shifted when I took the uniform off, but I went into overdrive going down a completely different and brand-new professional career path.

There were positives that came from that decision, though. I returned to school full-time to pursue a master's degree in social work. It was as if I were learning how to be both a civilian and a social worker simultaneously. That was a great time for me to learn who I was as an individual in my new role as a civilian. I highly recommend pursuing education post-military service because it gives you the time you may need to transition to civilian life and to gain connections in the career field you are pursuing without the pressure of meeting an employer's expectations. That time helped me learn how to feel comfortable as a veteran and communicate effectively with others, especially while trying to not come across as too demanding, or what

I've heard some refer to me as "abrasive." Communication and working with others outside of uniform is an art and you, as the artist, need practice in creating this.

Reflection: Having moved approximately ten times over my military career and as a military spouse combined, I began to focus on the aspects of my life that I could control upon arriving at a new location. It was important for me and my spouse to belong to a gym in the community that provided activities for our children and gave us an opportunity to stay physically and mentally healthy, and to find good childcare and schools for our children as well. Finding a gym was always the easiest of tasks. Being able to exercise and connect with others at the gym made it a great deal easier to tolerate all the things outside of my control.

Now finding childcare in general at many locations can be impossible. While living in Hawaii in 2018, prior to the pandemic, there was one point in time for a period of six months when all three of my children were each at different childcare centers at three separate military installations. That meant I had to budget an hour of time to drop all of them off prior to getting to work by 7:30am. I still do not know how I got through that time, but it eventually passed. During that period, I reminded myself that I would not allow the systems that continue to be a great difficulty for us to navigate, to stop me. I weathered the storm, and you can, too. I know that if something is important to us, we can find a way.

1. Have you moved to a new location and had to start over? What was that like for you? How were you able to overcome that transition?

____

____

____

____

____

____

____

____

____

3
MORE THAN A PRETTY FACE

---

*"If only our eyes saw souls instead of bodies, how very different
our ideals of beauty would be."*

— Anonymous

The perception of the military for many is that it is historically a male-centric organization and, as such, it is still saturated with ideals of chivalry (at best), chauvinism (not so good), and sexism (at worst). This environment can be compared to those employed in male-dominated industries, such as engineering, IT, construction, and trade programs, to name a few. All women who serve in the military, no matter their appearance, are treated differently and if you are a woman, you probably know exactly what I mean. Detractors to this reality want proof of this, but these are experiences I am referring to, much of the time, and thus lack direct, tangible evidence of specific treatment. It is a feeling that produces an invisible wound in many situations that often isn't acknowledged until a later point in life.

I know there can be special treatment for those that are attractive. I also think it is important to know that attractive people can be skilled, intelligent, and hard-working. I've heard many people in the entertainment industry say this, but I think this applies across industries. It's important to realize that these "pretty" women are not just there for the viewing pleasure of their peers; they are there to serve a purpose like everyone else. While growing up, this type of idealism was completely beyond my awareness. I started to gain an understanding of what that stereotype was during my time in the military.

While serving in the Army and stationed in Korea, around 2006, a special job position became available that required one to interview and, if hired, to leave their current position. For those of you who have not served in the military or served during this timeframe, there were not many times that you interviewed for a military assignment. One would receive a piece of paper, called military orders, telling you what your job was going to be and where it was going to happen. In that particular instance, it was one of my first post-undergraduate school interviews.

It was put out to all eligible candidates to interview and take the job if wanted. One of my supervisors told me they chose me to interview because I was a hard worker. I was around twenty-three years old at the time. I was so concerned with just doing things right that I was unsure how others viewed my work ethic. So those encouraging words gave me the confidence to proceed with the interview.

I ended up getting selected for the position and I was so excited that I called home to Upstate New York to tell my family the news. I remember a respected male family member saying, "Well, wouldn't you like someone that can do the job and looks good, too?" What? *"That's not why I got the job!"* I told myself. *"I was* qualified *to do the job!"* my inner voice insisted. But my family member's words created a spark of skepticism about my abilities that I wish I had never entertained or imagined. Nevertheless, taking that position changed the trajectory of my career, and, thankfully, the ones that selected me became my Army mentors. They have always been there for me, well past that assignment's ending.

Then, in 2009, I deployed to Iraq with my unit. We had a handful of females who were dispersed across different locations in Iraq. There were only two women at my site, on Camp Adder, including me. There were other women stationed at the same location from other units but not very many. Everywhere a woman walked, we were watched. Do you know how self-conscious that can make a woman?

For example, a soldier came to me one day and told me I was tied for number one for being one of the best-looking women on the post. *"I'm sorry, what? There is a ranking system, and all the men knew about it?"* I wondered to myself. So, I didn't have to be only concerned about my job, the main mission, but also this second mission going on behind the scenes. That made me want to isolate myself as much as I could while I still carried out my job to the best of my ability.

So, you as the reader may be thinking, *"What is the point in all of this?"* My point is to alert you to the fact that there are people out there who assume if you are good-looking then that is why you are wherever you find yourself to be. I have never once thought to say to a man, "You must have gotten this job because of how attractive you are." The bottom line is that women can do any job well no matter how they look. Women need to continue to work hard and stand up for themselves and each other when faced with this kind of discrimination. Likewise, women can educate the males they are raising and those they work alongside to put an end to this absurdity.

Reflection: There have been many times where people assumed my looks got me what I had in my life. For instance, I was given a company commander position straight out of my military school in 2009 which was unusual and quite difficult. Many military leaders want to know their junior leaders' capabilities before putting them in a position of such awesome responsibility, especially that of company command.

There was a male peer of mine that said, "Oh, you got that job because you are a female going to that type of unit and they want to put the males in these other kinds of units." It was implied that the units men were assigned to were of more importance than the units women were assigned to. Little did they know that my boss from a previous assignment had gone to the assignments manager to fight for me to have that position because of my abilities. The assignment manager told me, upon assigning me to this new position, that very few people have leaders calling to suggest a specific name and put in requests for certain positions.

1. Has there been a time when you felt your abilities were being questioned because of your looks? How did you handle the situation?

2. What words of advice can you pass on to another in a similar situation?

PART TWO

THE ESSENCE OF A MILITARY SPOUSE

Now, just as you may not have worn a uniform through military service, law enforcement, or as a firefighter, you also may have never been or currently be a military spouse. But you may relate to being in a relationship, as a spouse or family member, where someone moves for another's career. If you have done this, you might just know what it's like to have to start over with *everything*. If not, imagine what that might be like. Having empathy for others in these types of situations creates room for connection and understanding rather than indifference and disconnection. We can all gain from having empathy. This section touches upon the aspect of military spouses' lives around having to give up things, places, jobs, and people, to support their spouses' military career. Military spouses give up these aspects of themselves each time they move and somehow find the inner strength and knowledge from previous experiences, to start anew.

Reflection: Every time my family moved, there was something I had to put on pause for my spouse to be able to step into the next phase of his career. Each time that happened, he moved up the ladder in his career in a sense and I either stayed on the same step or took a backwards step in the new locations. The steps backwards often involved starting over in a new job as the newbie in that probation phase where I would be the last one to be granted the leave dates I wanted. Even if I wanted to take time off, I had no available leave balance; I left that behind with each job I relinquished.

Better still, because I was new, I was guaranteed the opportunity to work all the major holidays so that the permanent staff could continue to take the leave dates of their choice. In those situations, I gave up the possibility of climbing the ladder in the organization for which I was employed. I did, however, gain countless invaluable gifts that I would not have had had we stayed in one location. These gifts consisted of being able to undergo new professional experiences, constantly forging new friendships, and being exposed to new cultures.

1. Can you think of a time you started over completely for someone else? Maybe you changed schools as a kid, moved for a family member's new job, or returned to school to pursue a new career?

____

____

____

____

2. What was given up or left behind in this process?

____

____

____

____

____

3. What was gained through this surrender?

____

____

____

____

____

4
WIZARDESS

"You are unrepeatable. There is a magic about you that is all your own."

— D.M. Dellinger

Military spouses are magical, of course, all women are, but this section is to highlight this unique group of amazing women. Many military spouses have also served in uniform, and some still do. Military spouses are wizards. Better yet, they are *wizardesses*. Military spouses are the true wizardesses behind the curtain... making all the magic happen while most of the time not being seen or recognized. Yet they keep going strong for the greater good of our service members and our country. They have so many tricks up their sleeves that most of the time they make things happen before others even knew it needed to be done. I am amazed and in awe at all the military spouses I've seen persevere and thrive despite the countless obstacles stacked against them. They are a breed of their own, one that I am honored to belong to.

Military spouses will never be a carbon copy of each other. Each of us brings something special to the table. We all hold the priceless value of selfless service in us for the sacrifices made for our spouses. Those sacrifices may entail parenting alone while their service member is out in the field or has gone to another location for training, or off to a foreign land in combat, all with the knowledge that some of those service members may never return. Other sacrifices include making home repairs and car repairs alone, or even having a child in the absence of their military partner. No amount of gratitude can fill those voids. Even so, I want to thank all military spouses for all that they do. I have a strong inclination that our service members would be in a world of hurt devoid of the presence of their spouses.

Our service members would not be able to carry out their missions without the support of their spouses and if the service members are single, then often their immediate family members step into that support role. Military spouses help make their service member's missions possible by taking on the responsibilities of parenting, civic duties, and other obligations so that the service member can focus on their military duties without worrying about things at home. Much of what is done in support of our country's service members go without praise. That is why there is no better time than now to come together to support each other in our journeys and celebrate the strengths we spouses bring with us.

Reflection: There is not one military spouse whom I have befriended that has not mystified me in some manner. Whether it was gaining a position of authority in a work setting due to hard work, starting a new business that never existed in that location, working or going to school while at the same time raising children solo because a spouse was deployed, picking up the pieces to stand on her own to start anew after a divorce, or packing up a home and holding it together for her children after her service member passed away.

When I deployed to Iraq in 2009 at twenty-six years old as a company commander, I was single with no children. There was no inkling of wedding bells in my future, so I had no one back home to send care packages to my soldiers and me. My mother stepped in to fill that role and mailed care packages to all my soldiers for Easter that year. Some of those soldiers never received a single piece of mail from anyone other than my mother during that entire year-long deployment. That was so touching to me, and it affected those soldiers immensely.

Looking inward, I, too, can recognize the vulnerability and courage I put forth to keep pursuing and achieving my goals. I am proud of myself for continuing to identify ways I put myself first just as much as my spouse because our dreams are equally important. This precedence is then taught, and role modeled, for our children. Society collectively as a whole needs to work to shift this mindset that all our goals, men's and women's, are significant.

1. Who is one individual that comes to mind for you that has mystified you with their magic? What is it about them that you admire?

____

____

____

____

____

2. What do you also see in yourself that you are impressed by?

____

____

____

____

____

____

____

5

IMPOSTER SYNDROME

---

*"You don't have to be an expert. No one is expecting you to be an expert.
All you need to do is show up and be you."*

— Ruth Soukup

D o you ever get the feeling that you are not quite doing the military spouse thing right? This situation can be similar for spouses of individuals in positions of high responsibility and importance beyond the military. There are times when I have felt like an imitation of the real thing. When I conjure up an image of a military spouse, I think of someone actively engaged in the Family Readiness Group (FRG), volunteering in the community, homeschooling their kids, and rocking a side business. (The FRG is an organization created for the family members of service members in the Army to communicate happenings in the military unit, provide needed support, and volunteer opportunities to raise money for the military unit events.) I imagined the ideal military spouse pouring one hundred percent of their time into supporting the military.

When I think about that, I remember the military spouses I was exposed to while I served on active duty. They were the spouses of the higher enlisted and higher-ranking officers, and they always dedicated a great deal of time to their spouse's units. That image of a military spouse became ingrained in my mind, and I equated those efforts to the success of their service members. So, soon after getting off active duty myself, I tried to squeeze every ounce of me into the box that I imagined was expected of me as a spouse. I did not even consider if it would make me happy, just that I wanted to be the *perfect* military spouse for my service member. This was not something my husband had expressed, yet I was completely set on doing what I felt I was *supposed* to do for him, to fill those unspoken expectations.

So, along with getting employed, I also signed up for all the military events I could. I volunteered, attended meetings, and conducted fundraising efforts in the mornings before work. Those endeavors quickly lost their luster after I realized how much effort I was putting into it, but realized my effort was not as appreciated as I thought it would be. It was not as fulfilling as I had imagined because I was trying to be someone or something I wasn't.

I realized I had lost myself in that military spouse role when I was at an FRG function and I introduced myself by saying, "Hi, I am Major Kramer's wife." There was silence at that moment. Oh, my goodness, I had not even said my name! I was overwhelmed with embarrassment. I most definitely did not want to turn into one of those spouses that wore their husband's rank. That was another red flag for me. I knew I needed to find a way to support my husband's career so that he knew I cared about his success but also while developing a life of my own outside of him. I needed to create my own identity separate from that of being a military spouse.

The best advice I can give is to build your life the way you want it to be and fit the military spouse role into the cracks of that desired life where you can. Ask your service member what their expectations are of you when it comes to supporting their military career. The bottom line is that you will not be happy if you do not have something for yourself. When I was knee-deep in getting involved with everything, I did not ask myself why; I was too busy trying to be the *perfect* military spouse.

Take a moment to step outside the box to see where there is room for you. I know now that the lives I imagined of the military spouses I met while on active duty and the ideals I conjured up for my own role as a military spouse were not reality. Or at least, not the reality of most spouses. Now, when I am surrounded by other military spouses, I can see and feel my authentic military spouse self. I can relate to their victories, big and small. I know that we will not all be able to offer the same, but we all have something to offer.

Reflection: At that point in time, I had just completed my master's degree in social work and started to provide counseling to men and women in the community. Many of the women I worked with were military spouses themselves. Much of what they would share with me was about having to give up everything for their spouses' careers and not having anything for themselves. That was a lightbulb moment where I would see parts of myself in them. I was working yes, so that was me following my career passion, but all my free time was dedicated to my spouse and our kids but not me.

I started to make gradual changes to ensure I was filling my own cup of self-love, too. I continued to pursue my professional goals and ensured I carved out time to go to the gym and spend time with friends with and without our children. That was when I started to align with my true self. When we give our whole self to others, we block the gifts we could be giving to ourselves. When we pour more love into ourselves, there will be more love to pour out in unimaginable ways.

1. What do you have to offer to yourself, family, friends, coworkers, community, or even to the universe?

____

____

____

____

____

____

2. What is stopping you from putting that out there?

____

____

____

____

____

____

6

YOU ARE SHARING YOU

"Giving connects two people, the giver and the receiver, and this connection gives birth to a new sense of belonging."

— DEEPAK CHOPRA

Being a military spouse is extraordinary and unique, and so are you. Organizations you encounter may not know yet, but they soon will. You are special, and all the knowledge and experience you bring with you are invaluable. When you come to this new work setting, you bring all these wonderful parts of yourself. Most of the time, unfortunately, if you are a military spouse, you will only be there for two to three years and then move. Use this knowledge to ignite a sense of urgency and the importance of putting your skills to use. Now, we know that what we want is to leave each organization better than we found it. Sometimes this will not be perceived well.

The New Yorker and veteran in me tends to zero in on what is the right way to do things. When I say right, I'm not saying the only way, but the right way. The ways that are legally, ethically, and morally sound. There is always more than one way to do something right but never a right way to do something wrong. Some people will take your questions and suggested changes as insults even though you have the best intentions in mind. We are sharing our knowledge and want to, again, leave an organization better than we found it. When your conviction to make things right is met with resistance, don't give up; keep pushing. The path to success at times is lonely but remember the reason why you started.

Reflection: Times when I have spoken up against injustice occurring within organizations and advocated for those who had not found their own voices, recalls the image of the momentous task of female salmon swimming upstream to spawn. Like that salmon, swimming against the rough waters to get to their desired destination, they continue to push through despite the resistance.

I had my military spouse coworkers that came from the same waters and had migrated to these new waters due to military moves. We swam in the same water, had the same blood within us, and had the same desired location to swim in, too. We swam together despite the resistance we constantly experienced. We came out better because of this resistance and we survived. Those were uncharted waters for us. But just as in life, we go through uncharted waters to hopefully birth greatness within us, externalizing what we carry inside us. As women, we are here to not only birth children but to birth new life into our environments through our creations. Everyone that surrounds us can benefit.

1. Who are those people in your life that supported you when times were tough and enabled you to swim upriver despite the rough waters? How did they support you?

____

____

____

____

____

____

2. What can you say or do to thank them for the time they were there for you?

____

____

____

____

____

7

LOVE-HATE RELATIONSHIP

---

*"I have a love-hate relationship with losing. I hate how it makes me feel,
which is basically sick. But I love what it brings out."*

— Pat Summitt

We can all relate to the love-hate relationship we develop with the military, no matter the service, just the overall beast that it is. I can relate to this love-hate feeling both from having been a service member and a military spouse. From the service member's point of view, I have a love-hate for the negative experiences I went through and the things I missed. Most of all, I hate the time missed with loved ones. However, I have an overall love of the person I became through my service and that experience.

Another aspect of love-hate from the military spouse's point of view concerns the relationships we develop. As a military spouse, I've experienced bitterness toward my past self for how easily I could form relationships while in uniform. I did not have to work for relationships during that time. I moved somewhere new, and it was, "These are your friends, these are your coworkers, and this is your job." It was easy.

For military spouses, it was and is more challenging. But, through the hard work, anxiety, fear, sweat, tears, blood, and vulnerability, we developed our relationships. I am referring to the relationships with other military spouses, co-workers, moms of our children's friends, neighbors, daycare workers, hairdressers, nail technicians, teachers, and "tribe" friends. It wasn't easy and I would not give up those relationships for the world. That is love. The hate is the leaving.

Reflection: As a military spouse, I knew from day one that the military came first but I did not fully understand the heartache attached. There are the repeated *everythings*. Setting up the house, arranging school and childcare, doctors and dentists, and nail salons and hair stylists. There are also repeated blessings if you are open to seeing them. Don't give up. Make sure you always do something each day where you put yourself first to get through the heartache. Don't allow resentment to overwhelm you. Remember, you chose this life, too.

1. What are things you do to stay in the present moment to truly enjoy the relationships with those that you still have time with before one of you leaves?

2. How much effort do you give when you are with others to truly connect with them and what could you be doing differently?

8

THE ART OF MAKING FRIENDS

"What draws people to be friends is that they see the same truth. They share it."
— C. S. Lewis

Honestly, I wish I had the answer to this one. When stationed at Fort Bliss around 2014, I found myself in the perfect friend-making scenario. All the neighborhood couples were crowded together in one of the driveways of the street we lived on. I could easily meet all the ladies and my husband meet the guys, super excited as we had moved in about a month prior. The first question one of the ladies asked me was, "Do you work?" *Great, good going,* I thought to myself, *not, "Hey, do you have any kids?" or, "Where are you from?"* I gave an enthusiastic, "YES!" but it was apparent I gave the wrong answer—or at least not the answer they wanted to hear. It wouldn't have mattered if I added, "Did I mention I'm a woman, I like chocolate, wine, and shopping?!" What is up with the invisible wall that suddenly appears between women who work and those who don't work as if we no longer speak the same language?

Once you enter the workforce, there seems to be this battlefield of competition. *Do you have kids? How many? Do you (or did you) breastfeed? If so, for how long?* So much unnecessary pressure to conform to an ideal that only exists on social media or to a time that existed prior to women joining the workforce and having a voice. I found that the women who accepted me for who I was were those who were meant to be in my tribe.

I recall a time I had been saying goodbye to friends I had formed through a business networking group in El Paso called "Breakfast with Friends." A local member of the group mentioned how it was hard to make friends with military spouses because they always left. Since I know how hard it is to form relationships that must end due to moves, I want to say thank you to those "locals" who continue to open their hearts to military spouses. You become vulnerable through sharing your lives and families with us even if it is only for two to three years. Those years mean the world to us military spouses, veterans, and contract employees, and provide memories to last a lifetime.

One piece of advice I can give is: don't stop yourself from making friends. Put yourself out there. What have you got to lose? And what have you to gain? Find your fellow spouses who work in similar fields and build your tribe. If you are not in the best of locations, having that tribe to reach out to will carry you through that time. Friendships should not feel like a job, and they should not be one-sided. So, find those people who will reciprocate what you put out and that you can easily pick right back up with even after the passing of time.

When I moved to my newest location mid-pandemic in 2021, I decided to try the "blind-date technique" to try and make some new friends in the area. I created a post on social media saying that I wanted to meet other military spouses in the area at a specific public place for coffee. Just like the adage, "If you build it, they will come"—well, they came! I met some wonderful people at different stages in their lives and careers. But just like a blind date, I didn't have to marry all of them.

The downside I struggled with in that scenario was feeling the need to please those new contacts to keep these relationships and I put a great deal of effort into planning those engagements. That aspect of those relationships grew to be one-sided, but I had laid the groundwork at the beginning where the expectation was for me to do all that leg work. When summer break arrived, I decided to stop being the initiator. My phone went silent from this group for months: seven months to be exact. Some of those individuals started to initiate meetups which was refreshing for me since I was no longer having to do all the work myself. This experience taught me and continues to remind me how to create new relationships where equal efforts are put forth by all parties involved.

Now when I use the words "work" and "friendship" together, it is important to acknowledge that friendships are actually work. But you do not have to carry all the loads. I have friendships in my life that are so good they feel almost effortless. When you do meet your tribe, you learn to truly value the time you have together knowing that each day that passes is one less day you have together. This is true in all our relationships. But with military spouses, this is something that always stares you in the face. Time. When we start to form those real friendships, we ask each other, "When did you get here?" and, "When will you leave?" We want to know from the beginning to mentally prepare ourselves for that certain goodbye. I've always hated that about the military.

I'm blessed to have had a collection of military spouses that have touched my heart along the way. They are always with me even after we've all moved on to new assignments. These friends I refer to as my "seashell" friends. You know the beautiful shells with captivating imperfections that you find scattered on the beach. The ocean finds a way to shape and shine those shells. That ocean is our life with all the turbulence that comes with it. I'm lucky to have found these shells throughout my time as a service member and military spouse, along the beach of life.

Reflection: For me, most of my tribe friends materialized during the darker times of my life. It was as if the universe placed those people in my life just when I needed them. Also, if you think about it, a diamond cannot form without friction. If you can sit with a person and be with them through the friction, you will also be able to enjoy being in their presence in smooth waters. It is when things get tough that some people tend to jump ship.

1. Who are those "seashell" friends in your life?

____

____

____

____

____

2. What drew you all together?

____

____

____

____

____

____

____

9
YOU CAN LEARN A LOT FROM AN INTERVIEW

"Above all else, trust your intuition."

— Monique Glover

One thing that military spouses who are employed often do after each military move is go to job interviews. I have learned valuable lessons from interviews after the fact. I kick myself for not learning those lessons sooner. It took me eight months post-interview in the first scenario below, but I have now been able to embrace all that was learned through the experience. After spending four years in El Paso, it was now time for my family to Permanent Change of Station (PCS) to Hawaii in 2018. When I interviewed with a non-profit organization that serviced the homeless population, it would be my first time both employed in the Oahu community and working with that specific population. I was very eager to get my feet wet.

Toward the end of my interview for this organization with two of its highest management individuals local to the area, one male and one female, the female interviewer commented, "You won't enjoy your time here in Hawaii if you decide to take this position." Thinking back on this comment, I believe she did her coworker the favor of interviewing me but did not have the intention of hiring me. I believe that it was the male interviewer who selected me because of my qualifications. Either way, I should have listened to her telling me she did not want to select me based on her direct comment about not enjoying my time in Hawaii.

If any interviewer tries to talk you out of selecting a position when they called *you* to interview, I recommend not taking that position. In my situation, I instead took that phrase as a challenge and thought to myself, *"Challenge accepted."* But, boy, was she right; I did not enjoy my time in Hawaii while employed with that company. If you take a job at the start of a move and your job becomes your life, leave. And if you get into a dark place where you cannot see that happening to you, please listen to those in your life that know you best.

Now, this second example was almost identical to my experience in Hawaii but, for some reason, I guess I needed it to happen twice before I learned the lesson. When interviewing for a city behavioral health organization in Virginia, in 2021, I had similar red flags that came up during the interview process. The three interviews I attended with this organization seemed to go well until the interviewers started to tell me about other opportunities that were available within their organization. It was as if they had already selected someone for the position I wanted. They were just checking the box to be able to show that other applicants had been interviewed. Once I finally got into the organization, I was able to see that the jobs I interviewed for were indeed filled by individuals who were already working within the organization and had taken promotions. Then, of course, the management position I was not selected for had been filled by someone *from the area*. I previously mentioned in this scenario that my non-Virginian residency status had been my disqualifier. This second lesson only took me three months to learn before I was off to more interviews outside of that company.

It seems that there are many organizations out there that consider one's time in that organization as the main qualifier to continue to move up the ladder, with almost complete disregard for actual leadership abilities. This approach thus completely disqualifies other applicants with equal or greater abilities. I've seen individuals who do the bare minimum selected for promotions just because they have been with the organization for years. Why do organizations continue to accept the bare minimum as the standard? When this occurs, that is when newer employees, who continue to excel, move onto other employment opportunities where their hard work is acknowledged.

In my current position, I am employed with a company that I have worked for in the past and I know there are endless opportunities available regarding training and advancement opportunities. Unfortunately, this company needs to do better at transferring those employees who move due to military moves or because of spouses moving for their jobs. I had to go through two jobs prior to this new job. To get hired back into this specific government organization, I ended up taking a lower grade than what I previously held. This was a difficult thing to do but the pros outweighed the cons. You may find that there will be occasions when you move around that you may have to do just that, take a lower pay grade or lower salary, to get into the organization. But once you are hired, they may see you shine, which will most definitely afford opportunities that would not have been presented to you if you had not taken the chance.

Reflection: One interview question that I have grown to love and appreciate is, "If you were an animal, which would you be?" I've been asked this question at least twice but never gave much thought into the value of it until afterwards. I would be an elephant because of their great memory, their ability to lead the herd, and for their commitment to care for those in the herd. The elephant is large which is a comparison to the large amount of effort I put into my work and how much I care about the work I do. When I take on an endeavor, I tend to go all in, in a large way. I also care that no one on the work team is left behind when learning new knowledge or with work happenings. Lastly, I would not be a gray elephant, I would be made of colorful patchwork. The different patches would symbolize the experiences I have been through, all the opportunities and the obstacles, and the stitches around those experiences are the silver linings holding the wisdom gleaned.

1. Was there a time when you wished you had listened to your gut intuition during an interview? What was the intuition that you ignored?

2. What advice can you give yourself now to not make that same mistake again?

3. If you were an animal, which would you be?

IO

THE QUESTIONS NO ONE TALKS ABOUT

"Differences challenge assumptions."
— ANNE WILSON SCHAEF

Okay ladies, we all know that no matter how we present ourselves in an interview we will never be able to hide the fact we are military spouses, veterans, or someone from a foreign land or culture. Our resumes say it all. I have lost track of how many times I've been indirectly asked about my military spouse's status. Questions such as, "Curious, what brought you to this area? How long will you be here? Is your husband in the military?" I can recall a coworker asking me how long I planned to stay in Virginia right after I had gotten hired. That was quite comical in my situation because she had no idea that my husband was planning to retire from the Army at this point and that we were STAYING in Virginia. What is that saying again, "When we assume, we make an ass out of you and me?"

When my family knew we were going to make Virginia our forever home, my mother, sister, and brother-in-law decided to move to the area, too. We just happen to have a cousin living there, as well. One night when I had gotten together with my sister and cousin, we talked about all the transitions to the area. Interestingly, my sister was asked if her husband was in the military during an interview. She explained that she was shocked to be asked the question and wondered why it was even asked. The funny thing was that neither she nor her husband had ever served in the military. I said, "Well, because you look like a military spouse. I have been asked that in many interviews." My cousin then asked, "What does a military spouse even look like?" My response was, "When you do not look like the people living in that area, don't dress like them, don't talk like them, combined with your resume, it is a dead giveaway." In a way, we are almost always viewed as the outlier.

An example of this was when I went for an interview in Hawaii. I wore a nice dress suit because it was, after all, an interview. I walked into the lobby of the organization, and I started to see what I assumed were staff members. I let the gentleman greeting and signing people in know I was there for an interview. Staff members who walked by would ask if I had been helped. Most of them were wearing jeans and flip-flops or "slippers." Now if you have never been to Hawaii, you will quickly learn that this is a cultural thing, but in a work setting, I have always expected that you dress the part of whatever role you are performing. In social services, you should always dress in a way that says you are an employee and not a client. So, while waiting to be called for the interview, the volunteer in the lobby signing people into the building took a second look at what I was wearing and questioned, "You aren't from here, are you?"

Another instance occurred after I had just started working my second job in Hawaii; my direct supervisor told me she needed to meet with me one morning before work. The morning we met, we had about a one-minute chat. She said to me, "You can start wearing jeans to work, and don't come in so early." *Hmm, interesting,* I thought. Those were two things that simply were not *me.* I like to dress professionally in a professional setting, and I come early to work to be prepared for the day.

I was the outlier in that setting because everyone else wore jeans. I was not completely concerned with their work ethic because I was there to meet with clients and take care of them. When you go to a new location, it is important to get to know the culture of the area you are living in and to immerse yourself in it. But do not get lost in it, do not change who you are to simply blend in. Always be true to who you are and do not change that for anyone.

Those are examples of the, "what does a military spouse look like?" question. Now that you have been made aware of these questions, start thinking of your responses ahead of time—such as, "I am curious about why you are asking?" or, "Is this a requirement for the job?" as well as, "Do you ask your dentist to see their teeth?" (The last response was taught to me by my clinical supervisor.) Whatever your response, being a military spouse, veteran, or a new employee from another location has nothing to do with the job you are being asked to do. You may be an outlier, but that does not change the fact that you have skills and are amazing. Keep being you, keep doing you, and hold your head up high.

Reflection: There have been many instances where coworkers assumed I would not know how to handle certain situations because I was new to the organization. I have not allowed those assumptions to stop me from offering input. I have been able to analyze situations being faced within the present and think about how similar problems were handled in other locations where I've been employed. Many times, the input I offered helped my new place of employment develop new processes because I provided solutions they had not previously considered.

1. Is there a time when someone made you feel as if being from another location was a bad thing? What questions were asked of you?

____

____

____

____

____

____

2. What was it about you that caught the other person's attention? How do you view that aspect of yourself now?

____

____

____

____

____

____

II

TAKING THE REINS

"She was never quite ready. But she was brave. And the universe listens to brave."
— Rebecca Ray

It can be easy to fall into the mindset that, "I don't need to work." As a military spouse, I get it. It is hard to start over, and at times the military provides a pretty cushy lifestyle, especially if you are lucky enough to live near a beach. This can also be true for those not tied to the military who have spouses with professions that move around a great deal. This would be a similar situation where the one spouse working is the breadwinner, while the other spouse supports them from home. If you are the spouse who has given up your job more because of moving to support your partner's career, I can also see the argument to wait until your final move before putting yourself out there. That is a personal choice.

I learned very quickly after having my first child that I was not built to be a stay-at-home mom. I give loads of credit to the women and men who are. I learned that having a career that I loved was the thing that gave me purpose, energized me, and fueled me. Those remain true today. Having a career helped me get through long nights of nursing and being tired during the day because I was giving back to others. I also know now that the person I am in the present will create something more for my family tomorrow.

If the service member in the family is going to do twenty years of service, that will give you plenty of time to figure out if you would like to work and what exactly you would like to do. Life does tend to throw us curve balls, as we all know, so please don't make this your only plan for long-term financial security. When it comes time for you to choose a career field, I've learned the hard way that a career that pays a lot of money does not always make you happy. Do not just choose a career path based on the expected salary. One must dig deep inside to discover one's calling.

It is a good idea for the military spouse or supporting spouse to decide on that path at least three to four years prior to the service member separating or retiring from the service. That way you can be there to support your service member when they are transitioning from military service into their own civilian career. At times, this can be a very difficult and emotional transition. Having a career lined up as a military spouse helps to relieve stress and provide peace of mind to the separating or retiring service member. Then they can take the time they need to choose their new path after serving. We need to provide that security for our service members and our families. They made endless sacrifices for us, it is now our time to pay it forward. Be a spouse that elevates stress off your significant other, not one that adds to it. You'll both be happier.

Reflection: One thing that motivated me to buckle down into my career was what my husband had told me once. He shared with me that, "One thing you do by working is take a great deal of stress off me." By getting established in my career soon after arriving in what was our final military move, I gave my husband the opportunity to pursue a career he believed to be a calling for him. He started to gradually substitute teach on days off from work and started graduate school to gain a teaching license right after separating from the military. Whereas, had I not been employed, he would have been forced to take another job for the paycheck and not fulfill a dream of his.

1. What do you do for your partner or family member to help them during a transition they are going through?

____

____

____

____

____

2. How have they done that for you?

____

____

____

____

____

12

YOUR VOICE MATTERS

"Speak your mind, even if your voice shakes."

— Maggie Kuhn

I mean exactly what this title says: *your voice matters*. Do not ever once think that because of who you are or because you are someone new to an organization, your input cannot make a difference. *It can*. If you are a new military spouse or even a seasoned one, it will become obvious to you that the military does not acknowledge emotions. It has a "pull yourself up by your boot straps" and "suck it up and drive on" mentality. If emotions are holding someone back in their mission, they might hear, "Waiting on you." Whether the military thinks emotions are an important tool to use to gauge the effectiveness of their decisions or not, we know standing on the outside looking in, they are.

Consider yourself to be like a human portal to emotion. Our service members enter the military and are trained to not think about how they feel going into a situation or how losing a fellow service member impacts them because the mission must go on. Service members become almost like robots who act in the opposite way to how their bodies are instinctually built to respond as humans. When I provide therapy services for veterans who have separated from service, I work with them to transform from the "robot" mentality to learning how to accept emotions as they come instead of denying them. It is as if they are figuratively taking off that robot armor and learning how to be human.

Now there are many people who wear the uniform today that may have skepticism towards this viewpoint. They might proclaim that is not a true reality; the military culture wants its members to go to behavioral health and ask for help. I want to

41

believe this to be true, but even in 2023, I continue to hear the opposite from those wearing boots on the ground. It is so important for you as a spouse to speak up when you know your service member needs help, even if it is having a hard conversation with them or their leadership. Remember, you have your emotions telling you when something is not right.

An example of when I had to use my voice for my husband took place shortly before his retirement from the military in July 2022. In that situation, I was uncontrollably shaking. I had to breathe and process how to put into words the feelings I was experiencing because of a decision the military was making. My husband served in the military for twenty-one years with five combat deployments, so planning a retirement ceremony for him was very important to me and his entire family. We wanted a way to show our appreciation to him for the sacrifices he made for us and his country. Two weeks prior to the retirement ceremony, the military decided that due to "low participation," the ceremony would be postponed until that September, which was after the date my husband would have separated from service. That was a perfect example of the black-and-white thinking that occurs in the military that does not consider the emotions of those impacted.

This was my chance. When your body and your voice shake that is an internal message telling you *this is important.* Do not fail yourself or your service member by not using the voice you have been given to stand up for what you believe to be true. I used my voice to express how those actions went against what the military continued to say they believe in. I pointed out how the military loved to say they value families but, in this case, not when it did not benefit the service. I used my words to express how doing the right thing, holding a ceremony for someone prior to them separating from service and not afterward, allowed the service member to hold their head high and truly know and feel that their service was appreciated.

Believe me, when this does not take place and veterans learn how to feel and name their emotions, they recognize the anger deep down inside they hold for a military that did not value them as an individual. Use your voice for yourself, your service member, and for all the service members and spouses who have not found their voice quite yet. Be an example for them so that it will no longer have to be an example but the standard. So, to end this section on a positive note, the ceremony took place as originally planned.

Reflection: There was a time while serving in the military that I had to use my voice to stand up for something I truly believed in which also took place while I was deployed to Iraq. I was hosting a 15K road race called *The Boilermaker,* which is held annually in Utica, NY, right outside of my hometown. I had connected with the race organizers while in Iraq to see if they would be interested in sponsoring the race overseas to include sending race t-shirts. The race organizers were amazing, and they agreed to send a start and finish line banner, and approximately three hundred shirts for the runners.

I had decided that the shirts should go to the first three hundred runners that signed up to race. We had over four hundred service members sign up so not everyone would be able to receive a shirt. There was a male Non-Commissioned Officer (NCO) who demanded the shirts be given to the first three hundred race finishers. I could see this viewpoint but, being that I was the one leading this undertaking, I did not want this to be a repeated disappointment for those that tend to finish last. This same NCO corrected me in an organizing meeting in front of the base commander that we were going to hand the shirts to those that finished first. I remember this instance like it was yesterday. Something inside me was burning and my voice rose; "And I told you no, the shirts will be given to those that come to sign up first." The room was deathly silent after I spoke, and no one questioned that decision moving forward.

1. Was there a time when you experienced that gut-wrenching body shaking that forced you to use your voice?

2. Was there a time you did feel this but were unable to speak up? How can you use your voice today to advocate for yourself or others?

PART THREE

INGREDIENTS IN COURAGE

This section touches on those areas in our life that take courage from the root of our souls. I am more specifically referring to forgiveness, staying true to our values, defining expectations, sacrificing, and having standards. In a world constantly telling you how you should be and who you are, these aspects of life you need to define for yourself. Do not let anyone else define what these things mean for you or define who you are. If these were easy, we would not have to talk about them. Be kind and gentle with yourself. Use this section to start defining how these ingredients of courage show up in your life.

Reflection: For me, these areas of my life have become clearer and easier to define the older I get. When I was in college and much younger, I would tend to value others' time more than my own. I also did not always have standards when it came to the people I surrounded myself with. Now there are different qualities that I appreciate seeing in others that I was unable to see before, especially when a good portion of my college time socializing was around alcohol. Today, I value integrity, honesty, passion, humility, and ambition to name a few. When I can define the qualities that I value in myself and others, I have more confidence to set expectations, have personal standards, and make sacrifices that align with goal achievement. I do struggle with forgiving my younger self from time to time but remind myself I was doing the best I could at the time and know now that I can do better.

1. Which of these areas in your life do you struggle with the most?

____

____

____

____

____

____

2. What can you do or who can you talk with to gain more insight into this area?

____

____

____

____

____

____

____

13

FORGIVENESS

"True forgiveness is when you can say, 'Thank you for that experience.'"
— OPRAH WINFREY

Who comes to mind? What comes to mind? One person I would like to forgive is the younger version of myself. There are countless times when I catch myself with the thought process of, *"If only I listened more when I was younger,"* or, *"If only I did less of x-y-z when I was younger."* Remember, you are no longer that person and you are working hard now to reinvent yourself. It's important to love yourself and be patient with yourself. Love yourself for trying and for wanting to do better. Also, those mistakes turned into lessons that led you to where you are now. Don't stop yourself from all that is waiting for you. You will get there, you will see.

Reflection: One thing I would like to forgive myself for is for holding onto regret for staying in a long-term relationship from twenty-two to twenty-five years old to fulfill someone else's desires. Many times, parents pressure their children to find the right person, and this is exactly the pressure I experienced. All while moving across the country to learn how to be a soldier, I would get that reminder as if I would forget the expectation to procreate someday. That relationship was a distraction from my true self. I ended up breaking off that engagement and searching for myself through living my values, and eventually meeting my now husband three years later. We women need to learn how important it is to go out into the world to find ourselves before searching for someone else.

1. What is one thing you can forgive yourself or someone else for today?
    What would that forgiveness look like?

____

____

____

____

____

____

14
VALUES

---

*"Values are like fingerprints. Nobody's are the same, but
you leave them all over everything you do."*

— Elvis Presley

It's important to understand the things you value, why, and where they come from. For example, integrity, honesty, family, friendships, time, money, spirituality, or sobriety to name a few. Those values will come out in the work you do for yourself and for others. Our values come out in our words and actions. Make sure that your words and actions are aligning with your true values. This will help to bring you inner peace, influence the way you approach your work, and guide you in how you live your life.

I always ask myself, what I can be doing to be a better clinician, employee, and caregiver for my clients, employer, and family, now and in the future? Because I know that I strongly value the quality of work I put out, I can see how my work ethic gets passed onto the students I work with, my clients, and my family and friends. This value becomes like a fingerprint of mine left with those people I've interacted with, over time.

Not everyone will carry the same values as you and you will at times be met with resistance. Listen to your heart and it will help you not only stay aligned with how you live your values but also teach you to keep yourself connected to those that respect your values. It takes courage to walk away and separate yourself from those that you love who allow this value to negatively impact your relationship, but you must honor yourself above all else.

Reflection: Early on in my military career, I learned that it seemed as if the only emotion acceptable to outwardly display was anger. During my first assignment in the Army in 2005, I was exposed to different levels of anger, some more admissible than others. One day I was in a meeting with my commander and two of my peers. The purpose of the meeting was to provide updates to our boss on current projects. My commander was so dissatisfied with a status given by one of my peers that he both yelled and hurled a book from his desk directly at that peer. There was complete silence in that moment, and I sat there in utter shock.

After the meeting I approached both of my coworkers about reporting the incident and the one who had been hit said he would never report our commander because they both attended the same alma mater. In my mind, this was as if my coworker had given the commander an endless pass to treat him any way he chooses. No one should ever have the right to verbally or physically abuse someone, not in a professional or personal setting. I went onto report the incident without the support of my peers. The values I learned meant a great deal to me through this experience were respect and integrity. We have the right to be physically and emotionally respected by others and to have integrity to stand against those doing harm no matter a previous relationship with those committing wrongdoings.

1. What are the values that you live by?

____

____

____

____

____

____

2. How are you honoring your values in your life and in what way have they gone astray?

____

____

____

____

____

____

15
EXPECTATIONS

"You can do anything, but not everything."
— David Allen

Are you living up to your own expectations? If not, are those expectations realistic? Remember, *"You can do anything, but not everything."* No one can do everything; we are all human. We all have our talents and strengths, as well as our shortcomings. Do not get caught up in beating yourself up for things you have not been able to accomplish. Maybe those endeavors are not meant for you. It is your life's journey to figure out your purpose and how you will accomplish that.

Along with identifying your own expectations, it is important to gain an understanding of what the expectations are of your family. Being in a transitional family, whether due to military moves or new job assignments, can make this challenging. It is helpful to have discussions with your family to talk through which expectations are realistic. Our extended family will have different expectations than we do, and when those unspoken expectations do not align, conflict and resentment can arise. It is important to make expectations known on both sides to bring realities to light. We often want to please others and try to commit more than we already know we can. We can only do so much. We take care of ourselves when we learn to speak the truth.

I had a situation where the unspoken expectations caused a great rift in a relationship with a close family member that truly hurt me. This family member told me one day after having made our final military move that I had done my military service and military spouse life wrong. That hit me like a ton of bricks. The statement was then further explained with examples of what they thought I had done wrong. The feelings this family member shared were completely out of my awareness to include what they had expected of me. I went through a range of emotions in a period of one minute, including anger and sadness. I even felt terrible for the pain that a family member was experiencing, again out of my awareness. This conversation led to a rift in our relationship.

This situation leads to my original point about how important it is to share your feelings and expectations from the beginning. These things only get harder when time and distance are factors. Check in with your immediate and extended family members regularly. Ask what it is that they need from you to feel connected and let them know what you need.

Reflection: Most times, people carry the unspoken expectation of, *"Treat others how you would like to be treated."* Then later, one becomes upset when their actions are not reciprocated. When you begin to feel as if your relationship is more one-sided or that you are being used or taken advantage of, this is the exact moment that you need to speak up and say how you feel. Let's first assume that maybe this other party is completely unaware of their actions. But, once your expectations are expressed, it is up to the other party to show they respect you through their actions. If their behaviors do not change, you then are able to decide whether you want to stay in a relationship that in fact does not respect your desires.

1. Define what your expectations are for yourself in all areas of your life, such as with family, work, education, spirituality, and health.

2. Are you living up to these expectations? If not, what changes can you make?

3. Are there people in your life who place expectations on you that are not realistic?

4. How can you work together to refine them to work for all involved?

16
SACRIFICE

---

*"Challenges are what make life interesting and overcoming
them is what makes life meaningful."*

— Joshua J. Marine

You've probably been told this a million times, but think about the things you love that you are willing to put on hold to achieve something greater. Think about going back to school in addition to working, what are the television shows that you'll no longer be able to watch (at least at regularly scheduled times); bedtime tuck-ins that you may miss; and financial extras you enjoy on a weekly/ biweekly basis, like coffee or mani-pedis. Remember that the sacrifice you are willing to make today will help you accomplish your dreams for tomorrow.

I once had a military spouse tell me that she wanted to find a way for her family to make more money. She then said she was planning to return to school, but it would not be for herself. She planned to enroll in classes under her husband's name. Wait, what? Yep, you read that right. I inquired about why she would do that. She further explained that her active-duty military spouse could get more promotion points, get promoted, and make more money with that degree.

This was not the first time I'd heard of this being done where a military spouse completed a degree in their spouse's name. I remembered that while serving in the military, there were many soldiers who bragged about how their wives completed entire degrees for them in their names. So, at this point, I said to that spouse that she needed to go back to school for herself in *her* name. That way she could have a degree in her name and make more money for her family. Education is one thing no one can take away from you. Ladies, please stop going to school for someone other than yourself.

Reflection: I recently returned to school to pursue a Doctor of Philosophy (Ph.D.) in social work. This is an opportunity to both further my education and advance in my career. I have a strong desire to give back to the profession through research, to teach, and to step into leadership roles. After completing the first semester, I've been able to reflect on how demanding, time intensive, and emotionally exhaustive the time has been. I last went to school ten years ago in 2014, so it has been a shock to my system. I recall a couple nights during this past semester where I would be sitting at my dining room table working on a statistics test at midnight, class slides scattered everywhere, and tears running down my face. In those weak moments it could be very easy to just throw in the towel. I constantly reminded myself this challenge is part of the process. If I give up, I will stay where I am professionally. My spouse and my mom found ways to help take on some of my personal responsibilities to afford me the ability to focus on my schooling. I highly recommend that when you have a goal you are working to achieve that seems insurmountable, lean on those closest to you to assist you along the way. I know the sacrifices in the moment may seem unbearable, but they will not last forever.

1. What is one goal that you have that would require a great amount of sacrifice to accomplish?

____

____

____

____

____

2. What stops you from completing this goal?

____

____

____

____

____

17

STANDARDS

"The standards you set determine the life you get."

— UNKNOWN

Early on in our lives, standards are set by others whether it be by our parents, siblings, teachers, friends, or coworkers. Then, the older we get and the more experience we gain, we start to understand what standards are and begin to define, clarify, and perfect the standards we hold for ourselves. Your standards must be higher for no other than yourself. I've had clients say that their standards are higher for other people than for themselves. You deserve to hold yourself to a highly achievable and realistic standard. You can make changes to your standards at any time, but they should aid with aligning your behaviors to achieve personal or professional goals you have set for yourself. Remind yourself that even if you establish standards, you must put them into action through living them; nothing changes unless something changes.

Reflection: Two standards that are incredibly important to me are honesty and authenticity, telling the truth and being who you say you are. These two attributes usually go together because it is difficult to live one without the other. I had a friend whom I served with early on during my military service that showed me she did not live by these standards. I truly cared about her and wanted to give her the opportunity to show me otherwise, but I had to draw the line at some point. Knowing when to draw that kind of line in your life may not always be easy.

I visited with this friend one time while we were living in different states, when a work trip brought me to the city she was living in. She was attending graduate school at the time, and I met her out one night while she was with some of her classmates. Her friends asked me how we knew each other. When I mentioned we served in the Army together their faces stared back at me dumbfounded. My friend did not confirm this information and it became crystal clear that the image she wanted to portray was the life of a southern bell who would not have been caught dead wearing a uniform. This was when I saw she was not being her true authentic self.

This friend then lost my trust when she said she could not attend my wedding due to the passing of her grandmother. There was an elaborate story around the details of having to schedule this funeral for family members who wanted to attend. I did not get lost in the details and accepted the situation at face value. It was not until two years afterwards, over lunch, that this same friend questioned the date of my wedding. I was flabbergasted that someone could forget the date their grandmother passed away, which was the case for her. If she had just told me, "I cannot come to your wedding," I would have accepted that no matter the reason. But since the reason that was provided was based on a lie, I could no longer trust her, and chose to end that relationship.

1. What do your standards say about you?

____

____

____

____

____

2. Do you fully embody your standards? If not, what changes can you make to truly live those standards now?

____

____

____

____

____

PART FOUR

IN A HELPING PROFESSION – THE INTANGIBLE BLESSINGS IN OUR WORK

There are important aspects of the work done as a mental health professional that are not visible. There is energy in being this kind of professional. The way they interact with clients and do their work is an art. Unlike how one may have a recipe for a favorite cake, there is no recipe or quick fix for this work to help clients understand how they got to where they are in their life. This analogy used with the therapy profession can equally be applied to occupations like hair stylists, personal trainers, or physical therapists. There are set times for hair treatments, workouts, and physical therapy exercises, for the reason of achieving optimal results. By shortchanging the standards of these professions, you would only be shortchanging yourself.

I had a client ask me once to do a ninety-minute assessment in thirty minutes because that was all the time they had. This was a reflection of how they were living their life: they were clearly not giving the full time and attention required for their mental health, which would only hinder them in the end. I told them, "No, come back when you can make the time." The work put in as a professional or a client cannot be cooked in a microwave, so to speak. Sometimes this work is like sitting in the slow cooker all day long on a low setting. You gradually smell the change in the food cooking just as you will start to gradually feel the burn in yourself. The work done in therapy cannot be rushed.

Whether you directly serve clients or not, you still need to show up for your employers, subordinates, coworkers, or customers. In addition to how we show up for those we work with, it is equally important how we show up for ourselves. This impacts how stakeholders and those outside of our fields view us, as well as our society at large. There is a grand ripple effect that comes from our work. Do not shortchange yourself or those you serve. My hope is that this section will help you to see why allowing the process to happen besides manipulating it, is necessary.

Reflection: I believe that the people we serve and work alongside deserve the best version of ourselves, and this version will not be the same all the time. We have bad days, just like our clients or employees. But how we show up for them is extremely important. I try my hardest to dress nicely by ironing my clothes, wearing makeup, doing my hair, and putting on jewelry. I want the way I look to give a silent message that it is important for me to be here for them and that they are worthy. I know this makes lasting impressions on people so even on the days when I feel sluggish or under the weather, I remind myself of the things I've heard in the past. I had a coworker say to me, "Anne, you just look as if you put effort into the way you look." I had a client say to me, "You have motivated me to care about the way I look." When you make the effort to take care of yourself it feels good. This may seem like something small, but it does have a ripple effect on our day and on others.

1. How are you causing a ripple effect in the individuals you work with
   or in your organization or community?

____

____

____

____

____

2. What is the lesson coming from this ripple?

____

____

____

____

____

____

18

MAGIC DUST

"To inspire people, don't show them your powers. Show them theirs."
— ALEXANDER DEN HEIJER

There is no magic dust that falls on me or my clients when they walk into my office. The therapy room is practice for when clients leave the room and then put the skills they learned within therapy into action. If I do not think my client will know how to apply the skills learned on their own, I must find ways to ensure they will. For example, I had a client who was new to using technology. I worked with them to develop coping cards or instruction cards that went step-by-step with logging into their phone, selecting the proper app they needed to use, and how to address an email to a specific recipient. I approached their progress outside of my office much like a child learning to crawl, walk, and then running. I cannot give my clients a run task that they did not first know the how to crawl step. If we do the task for them, we are keeping them stuck.

As a clinician, it is imperative that I uncover my client's expectations of therapy. Just as in other professions, such as a Realtor, one asks for their client's expectations with buying a house. In my realm, I have found that clients come to therapy for multiple things such as to vent, to problem solve, find answers, or to have "the answer" given to them. I find it helpful to remain curious with my clients and to remind them that they have the answer within themselves. As the therapist, I am there to help them find it and to instill life skills in them so that they can learn how to live for themselves on their own. Exploring a client's expectations will help them to discover what it is that they are looking for. Again, this applies to all professions: deep down the answer is in there.

The real magic for me comes from the work I do with my clients, to help them discover the answers and to live those answers. They will learn to trust and embrace their own feelings and to use them as a guide to move forward. In my professional experience, the masterpiece at the end of therapy will be my changed clients. The work of art was always inside them, it just needed to be called upon, cheered for, and believed in by someone and then by themselves. The masterpiece is the work of art I helped to create but also the hard work the client put in to developing their assertiveness, confidence, and empathy. Just as I, as the therapist, was like a tool used by a client to get to that better version of themselves, the same is true for you with your clients, customers, or employees. You are the apparatus that gets the individual to the next level they desire to achieve. This is no small feat. That is magic.

Reflection: There are so many people in my life who have aided me in finding my magic. All the people that have expressed appreciation to me for something I had done, gave me a listening ear, or said they believed in me, sparked my magic. People have given me thank you gifts as well, but it has always been the words given to me by others or the way they made me feel in the moment, that have left imprints on my heart. Those loving acts have given me confirmation to keep going and inspire me to mentor social work students when I can to give back to the profession.

1. Who in your life helped you to find your magic?

\
\
\
\
\

2. How do you continue to use that magic to grow?

\
\
\
\
\

3. In what ways have you lost your magic?

____

____

____

____

____

____

____

19

WHAT IF I DON'T KNOW EVERYTHING?

"Start where you are. Use what you have. Do what you can."
— Arthur Ashe

This section applies to anyone working in a field within a profession that is new. For example, I've been asked many questions by interns and mental health professionals working with the military population that have had no military service or connection. Most have expressed in some way, "I've never served, I'm worried about that." First, I want to say thank you for choosing this path to serve others if this is the path you are on. I believe that the most important aspect when choosing a population to work with is that you want to be there. For instance, having served in the Army does not prepare me for all the military lingo that may come my way when working with veterans. That just means I know possibly half of the lingo that an Army soldier may use. All the other services have their own terminology and a lot of the different branches within the Army have their own lingo.

Since you and I will never know all there is to know about everything our clients, coworkers, or customers talk about or are going through, it is okay to ask them. If you do not understand what they are talking about, ask them to educate you. I encourage you to do your own research as well. This shows them that you are empowering them to own their stories. We are modeling how to be vulnerable by putting ourselves out there so that they do the same when they are unsure about what they are facing. The bottom line is that we will never know everything there is to know about being a clinician or about any career field for that matter. We must always remain curious, be aware that we do not know everything, and continue to educate ourselves as we go.

65

Reflection: I had a Vietnam veteran tell me from the beginning of our time together in therapy that I did not know what it was like to be deployed or know what he experienced in Vietnam. I explained to him that even if I had deployed to Vietnam, we would have had a different experience. I told him he was correct in saying that and asked if he could share with me what that experience was like for him. He was initially taken back from my response as if this was a response he had never experienced. I could see the tightness in him loosen right before my eyes. His voice calmed and he then taught me from that point forward what it was like for him to go into battle. I was relieved that he was receptive and honored that he shared his account. This gave him the opportunity to claim his story while being in control of it. I was surprised one day when he told me he enjoyed our time together and we were both sad when it ended.

1. Think of a time you went out on a limb with a client, customer, or even an employee and told them you did not know the answer. What was that like for you?

____

____

____

____

____

2. Were you surprised by the way they responded? Did this vulnerable action bring you closer together in any way?

____

____

____

____

____

____

20

YOU ARE NOT FOR EVERYONE

"No matter how hard you dance, not everyone will clap."
— Joan Erikson

This was one of the best pieces of advice that I received from my clinical supervisor. I was in one of those moments where I struggled with a client not making progress and my supervisor said to me, "Anne, you're not everyone's therapist." This was so right and the way he said it to me solidified everything I learned in graduate school about the therapeutic relationship. Just like we cannot be friends with everyone, we are not going to click with all our clients, coworkers, employees, or customers. When we feel that, it is up to us to bring that to light. If it is appropriate, ask the person in question how they feel about their relationship with you. If this is not something that can be worked through, then refer them to someone who may be a better fit. I cannot keep a client on my caseload without a strong therapeutic relationship because it doesn't do either of us any good. Also, a client, coworker, and certainly an employee or customer, may never share their feelings about you until you ask. This is one of those situations where you really do need to trust your gut. If you're feeling it, it's highly likely they are too.

Reflection: I've used this lesson learned many times since this conversation took place with my supervisor in 2017. I've asked my clients if our relationship was somehow impacting their ability to make progress in their personal goals. Each time I asked there was this moment of shock or even revelation that someone how increased their understanding of the importance of the work we were doing. It was as if I were able to communicate in a new way, "Hey this is important, we are not just here to check a block." I wanted them to understand that if it was me standing in the way figuratively of them being able to make progress, then I was going to move out of the way literally.

1. Is there a time you used your gut feelings in determining the strength of a relationship you were in or are currently in?

____

____

____

____

____

2. How did you use that internal pull to either strengthen your relationship or close the door on it?

____

____

____

____

____

21

MAKE SURE THEY HEAR YOU ROAR

"'Cause I am a champion, and you're gonna hear me roar."

— KATY PERRY

When you start a new job or meet a new employee make sure to introduce yourself confidently and with pride. Please do not say I am "just a" fill-in-the-blank. In my case, I caught myself saying, "I am just a social worker," and I thought, *Wait. What? Why did you say that?* In my career field, for example, it can be intimidating to work with doctors in certain settings, such as in a hospital, or with CEOs or managers, but you need to realize that your role is important, too. We all have different skill sets with different degrees, certifications, and experience. We all have a seat at the table for a reason.

If you are working on a multidisciplinary team, you may be the only social worker, psychologist, licensed professional counselor (LPC), licensed mental health counselor (LMHC), marriage and family therapist (MFT), or criminal justice professional. Just as in a lawyer's office, there are paralegals, legal secretaries, records clerks, accountants, and lawyers to name a few. Each employee is an integral part of the team. Be the expert in your role. You represent that profession. No pressure, but if you do not fully know your job or current state laws regarding your profession, now is the time to learn them.

When I say let them hear you roar, I mean let them hear you stand your ground when necessary. As a mental health clinician, I will work with many individuals that have a business mindset that strictly pays attention to numbers and dollar signs. Those individuals are not always interested in hearing about the justifications behind the rights and wrongs concerning clinical practice. They also may not care

69

to hear why I, as the clinician, am choosing to discharge a client and it is not the client choosing to leave. When you stand your ground, going against the grain and making that hard turn because it is ethically the right thing to do, make sure your decision is heard. Do not back down.

I recall an incident when I worked at a psychiatric hospital in an outpatient mental health setting running a Partial Hospitalization Program (PHP). This is where an individual comes in for therapy five days a week for a minimum of two weeks. In this setting, a patient continued to relapse using an illegal substance and I decided that the patient needed a higher level of care. Therefore, the patient needed to either be discharged from my program or transferred to an inpatient setting. My supervisor, with a business background and an MBA, insisted that the patient complete the authorized insurance days before making decisions about transitioning their care. I explained the reasons behind my decision and said if I were not allowed to make a clinical decision that was under my license, I would contact my malpractice insurance to discuss the situation.

My supervisor informed me that I could not do that. I further explained that I work for the state just as much as the hospital and that I would contact my malpractice insurance if I saw fit. Again, do not let someone without the appropriate background tell you what you can or cannot do with your license or within your area of expertise. The very next day I was asked to brief the CEO of the hospital on the situation. That specific CEO had both a clinical background in social work and a business degree. After the briefing on the case, the CEO agreed with my decision, and shortly after, my supervisor was removed from her position.

There were many lessons learned that day. One lesson was the importance of listening to the people that work for you that have specialized training and expertise in their area of work. We can learn from our coworkers and become better leaders from doing so. A takeaway for you as the reader is that there will be times when your expertise will be used to both educate and assist those in other disciplines in making decisions that, in turn, directly have an impact on the work you do. Some of those other individuals are the employees, supervisors, or managers that work in the financial offices that directly fund your services. If something does not feel right, it probably is not. Just make sure that you express how you are feeling and document when necessary. You can also look towards outside resources to assist you in working through dilemmas such as calling your malpractice insurance, a supervisor within your profession, or a mentor outside of your job. Even those of us that are independently licensed in a field or are fully qualified lean on our coworkers when a situation does not feel right. It is always best to err on the side of caution to work to prevent unnecessary mishaps. We owe our patients, clients, and customers the level of care that best meets the needs of their condition.

Reflection: When faced with ethical dilemmas in a work setting, when a client is being affected, I ask myself whether I would want a family member or friend of mine to go through this experience? If, after changing the perspective of the way I am looking at a situation, I still arrive at the same outcome in my decision, I stick with my gut.

1. Whether you work in a helping profession or not, has there been a time you spoke up in a situation with an unfavorable opinion because it did not feel right? What was the situation and what were the feelings coming up for you?

____

____

____

____

____

2. How did this brave action change you or change the environment you were in for the better?

____

____

____

____

____

3. Maybe there was an instance where you wanted to use your voice but were unable to. How have you strengthened this part of you have confidence in yourself to address similar situations in the future?

____

____

____

____

____

22

GRIEVING PROCESS

*"When I am brave enough to say goodbye, I'll use
the wings you gave me and away I'll fly."*
— CELIA MCMAHON

We all know that grieving is a real thing, our emotions do not end at goodbye. Just like the way we may feel with friends and family, either happy or sad to say goodbye, it can be equally the same with our clients, customers, community partners, or patrons on the receiving end of our services. As military spouses, veterans, and travelers, most of the time we have been the one initiating the goodbye because we are the ones leaving.

People may try to find the negatives of having a military spouse, contractor, or temporary employee getting connected to clients, customers, or partners in the community knowing from the beginning that they will be leaving in two to three years. But there is so much good that can come from allowing temporary employees to be in the lives of those they serve if even only for a short period of time. For me as a clinician, the relationship with a client starts out as an emotional dumping ground and, at times, as an emotional punching bag. I bear the pain clients feel and the pain of their families. I learn through those experiences and set boundaries with clients, and in doing so, I teach them through interaction. I coach my clients on what is acceptable in relationships, how to communicate needs and emotions, and most importantly, how to love. My limited time in one particular place does not hinder this relationship.

This is interchangeably so for other professions such as with a financial advisor. A client may come in with debt because of their irresponsible behaviors around

73

spending money. The financial advisor would educate and assist the client in setting boundaries around their spending habits to achieve their financial goals. By teaching one how to implement these important life skills and to continue living by them independently, the financial advisor is helping their client to build a healthy relationship with money and to have self-respect. This goal could be achieved in one visit or from multiple visits, but the time that financial advisor has remaining in their position does not stop the financial advisor from being an effective advisor in the moment.

So yes, as a military spouse, contractor, or short-term employee, providing a space for growth, for even just a short time—provides opportunity for lessons that can be sewn into the hearts of our clients or customers that will last a lifetime. Another lesson we can teach our clients, customers, or community partners, is how to say goodbye in a healthy way. We do not leave without saying goodbye, or as a mental health clinician, without patching up the wounds that were open when the therapy relationship started. There will always be pieces of pain inside us that need re-patching along the way. Hopefully, our clients, customers, or community partners will have learned how to trust and will be able to reach out for help again.

Just as my clients can benefit from having a military spouse, veteran, or traveling heart in their lives for a fleeting period, so can employers. This new employee could be just the fresh breath of air that your organization needs. They might be able to help you to see all the aspects of your company that need attention that the long-term employees have decided to turn a blind eye to or believe, "That's just the way it is."

The part about the relationship with employers that I grapple with is how some think that it is because you may be staying in an area for a couple of years that they have you as an employee for that whole time. The way I see it, employers need to work just as hard to keep us. We are not a guarantee. I encourage employers to learn to truly appreciate not only their military spouse employees, contractors, and short-term employees, but all their employees because when they do not, they are simultaneously hurting those they serve as well. These nomad employees have a great deal to offer and want to be heard and respected just as equally as the employees who have been there for years and may never leave. If this is not the case, they will go where their skills are most appreciated.

Reflection: When I worked in a homeless shelter in Hawaii that served veterans, it was my role to start a mental health program within that organization. I remember the clients I met thanking me for listening. It became very clear almost immediately that this was something they had never experienced in the shelter and some of these veterans had been in the shelter repeated times. One veteran told me he was used to being told what to do and never being the one telling his story.

Even though my leadership acknowledged they received positive feedback for the program I started, it was evident that the higher-level leadership would never recognize it. There were two lead employees that had been employed with the company for many years and the higher-level leadership said in a meeting one day that one of the two employees is the one running the organization and the other one is the face of the organization. It was apparent the establishment did not see other employees outside of these two as integral players but merely as disposable pawns on the board. The grieving that took place for me was in saying goodbye to the clients I served at that shelter. It was hard to leave knowing that the service I provided was greatly needed but reminded myself that I needed to be a part of an organization that recognized me as an indispensable player.

1. Are there instances that come to mind for you where you made a tremendous impact on those you served in a short amount of time? What were those efforts you put forth?

____

____

____

____

____

2. With new employers, how do you know whether you are being treated as a true part of the team? When you are sure that you are not, how long before you leave?

____

____

____

____

____

23

W.W.A.D.
(WHAT WOULD ANNE DO)

"All the flowers of all the tomorrows are in the seeds of today."

— INDIAN PROVERB

All your experiences being employed as a nomad woman will not be bad. If you work in a helping profession, I am sure you must know this by now, but most people come into the profession with a desire to help others. Sure, the helping profession could refer to one who serves in the medical field, but it can also refer to any career field where you as the professional are the link to bringing a client or customer to their best state. That link could be a professional who works as an artist, a nail technician, a hair stylist, or as a masseuse to name a few. The rewards you get from that kind of work are priceless. I live for those "ah-ha!" moments my clients reach through therapy. The moment things start to click for them, things start to line up, and they start meeting their goals. Those moments where they put all their trust in you and break barriers, especially the ones they never thought they could achieve are the best moments. They start believing in themselves when there may have been no one in their lives that did before. If you are afforded the chance to help create that in your clients, employees, coworkers, or customers, I am excited for you.

This brings me to the title of this section. One day in my therapy group room some of the group members were chatting before the group started. They got my attention and said to me, "Anne, you know those bracelets that say, 'What Would Jesus Do?' We need bracelets that say, 'What Would Anne Do.'" This group had me cracking up laughing and of course, this piqued my interest. They further explained that every time they were struggling with something, they would ask themselves, "What would Anne say?" I joked with them, saying, "Ah, I see you are learning."

77

This story should hit home to you about how important your job is. Therapy is not just what happens in the therapy room, and the same goes for all other professions. It is everything that happens when your clients, employees, coworkers, or customers leave your room. If those you interact with start to think *before* making decisions, that is progress. It starts with the seeds that you planted. Keep on planting those seeds and watch them grow. They will be the literal fruits of your labor.

Reflection: Just as our positive interactions in our work influence others greatly so do our negative interactions. The negative interactions can be felt with a greater impact and can either overshadow the positives or completely wipe them out. I remember a client explaining to me after a group therapy session that they did not like how I addressed their issue during the session. I greatly appreciated their ability to advocate for themselves and valued hearing their perspective. It was not my intention to come across the way they experienced my words, but I was able to gain an understanding about why they had. This is a situation where the client could have left holding onto their anger without repairing the rift my words had created. We both gained insight through discussing the hurt that arose in session allowing for the seeds that had been planted in session to continue to grow well after that time had passed.

1. How have you seen your efforts show up in those that you work with whether it is your coworkers, employees, customers, or clients?

____

____

____

____

____

2. Do you remember how that felt the moment you realized you were the individual that gave the push, the tug, the kind word, or the silence they needed to take those steps? Where have you seen those seeds grow?

____

____

____

____

____

PART FIVE

AS A MOTHER

You have been blessed with this grand ability that no man can take from you, to bear a child and be a mother. This section is for those who desire to be a mother or whatever their heart desires. This is our human right to decide what we want to be. Not all women will have the opportunity to carry a child, whether due to not finding the right match, infertility, or by choice. It is a monumental responsibility to be a mom, whether it is through childbirth, fostering, or adoption. My desire for you is to feel confident to show up in your role as a mother and in all other areas of your life.

Reflection: I never realized the magnitude of responsibility that came with the title "mom," which I know now is a sacred responsibility. When I first became a mom in 2013 with my son, it was as if seeing him for the first time was like a spark into this new dimension of life that I had never been to before. I saw life in a new way as if I now where able to understand, "Wow, everything connects for a reason." I gained a new awareness about the great importance of the little things, such as taking time to notice a change in one's appearance due to aging and asking how one's day was. These things can seem little at times, but they are truly important. These were phenomena I thought I knew were of value, but it was as if had been glazing over them up until stepping into this new role of motherhood. This new role also increased the value of important tasks making them even more serious and adding levels of consequence. I am referring to matters such as the significance of truly being present in situations and to ensure that the words you say really do match your actions. Being a mom has helped to put time into perspective in that we do only have a limited amount of it and that we need to do the best we can with the time we have.

1. In what ways can you start showing up more for yourself? Not just in your role as a mother, but for who you are as an individual?

____

____

____

____

____

2. What example do you want to set for your child or the children in your life?

____

____

____

____

____

3. How has becoming a mom in any way in your life, changed the way you view things?

____

____

____

____

____

24

MOTHERHOOD AND A CAREER

"Having children just puts the whole world into perspective.
Everything else just disappears."

— KATE WINSLET

Notice the word *and* in this chapter title. Yes, you can have both. I decided this was an appropriate topic to broach here because I do not think enough people talk about this. I remember when a fellow graduate student asked for advice during a class about having children while in school. The professor replied, "It would be best if you are planning to have a child while in graduate school, to give birth in June." Woah. If we could all only be this lucky.

Then, my mom gave me the best advice when she told me that there was no right time. This was something I reminded myself of constantly before I had my first child because I was clinging to the idea that if I had a kid, what would happen to my career? I feared I would lose sight of it or that it would be impossible to stay on the track I was on. Since I was in my first year of graduate school when I was thinking of having a child, I considered the advice from my college professor and my mom. I tried to become pregnant so that my child would be born in June. I guess the stars aligned for me because that dream became a reality.

My son was born in June 2013, and I am thankful things worked out the way they did. I learned during that summer break of graduate school that I loved my new role as a mom but that I still had the desire to pursue a career in social work. Thank goodness I had the fall semester scheduled for the following September as a force to push me back out into society. I was in a funk, adjusting to motherhood and from losing a family member that same summer. I also had a new motivation, my son, to keep pursuing my dreams.

Going back to my second year of graduate school was difficult. It was hard to leave my son. There was this cloud of guilt that I was leaving him and allowing other people to parent him. But as a military spouse or in a traveling profession, being away from family is a reality for most families, if not all. We learn to rely on the caring people in society to help us. Especially since most military spouses or women on the move do not live in the same town, state, or even country as extended family. Whoever coined the term, "It takes a village," was most certainly right.

Now, beginning a career while pregnant was not easy. I was pregnant with my second child when I graduated with my master's degree. Looking back on the interview process I embarked upon when my family PCS'd from Virginia to El Paso, I was determined to find my first paying job as a social worker. I was now close to being five months pregnant and feared that if I did not lock in a job right away while I was still small in the stomach, it wouldn't happen until after giving birth. I had a timeline mapped out to get the clinical license which takes a minimum of two years to obtain after graduation. I did not want to waste that valuable time.

Going to interviews pregnant was very frightening. This was pre-COVID, when all the interviews were in-person. I had thoughts going through my head that employers would take one look at me and not want me. I do know that a lot of these thoughts were from my judgments of myself and of how I had viewed pregnant women in the military while serving. It was as if one had to be 100% available for the military and of course, if you are pregnant, you are not fully available for all the needs of the military. My own experiences have helped me to be more empathetic and to remind myself to not judge others on their journeys. I know I've made plenty of mistakes and would hope I would not be judged but coached and mentored through those mistakes.

I had two interviews when I arrived in El Paso, and both employers offered me a job. The first interview was with a private for-profit practice, and it was with a female nurse practitioner. The first question I was asked by her was, "When are you due?" This question was not asked in an, *"I'm happy for you!"* tone. I was speechless. My younger self told the employer when I was due and that was the only thing asked about my pregnancy. I do not remember what else was talked about because I was filled with embarrassment. I basically heard the "Wah-Wah" Charlie Brown tone at this point. The nurse practitioner offered me a position that was ten hours a week and I do not know if my pregnancy prevented me from being offered a full-time position. I do know that the question asked about my pregnancy helped me to decide this was not the right employer for me.

The second interview was for a for-profit psychiatric hospital and the interview was also with a female clinician. There were no questions asked about my pregnancy and thirty to forty hours per week were offered. This was a game-changer for me.

I was thrilled that I silenced my thoughts to show up and put myself out there despite being five months pregnant.

If you are pregnant, please, use my lessons learned and push yourself to keep going. Keep going to school, keep going to work, and keep showing up to those interviews. Any good employer will see you for who you are and for what you have to offer, and not just as a pregnant woman. Don't hide this. Be loud and proud. Women shouldn't be ostracized for something that their body is meant to do. Let's collectively, as women, break this cycle of allowing men and women to shun us for being pregnant and instead, be supportive of each other.

Reflection: One irrational way I used to perceive pregnant women while serving in the military was thinking that they must being using their pregnancy status to get out of something, such as doing certain work tasks or to be excused from going on a deployment. This belief is coming from a younger version of myself before I had children. I now know that yes; it is possible that a woman could be doing this, but it is also possible that they are wanting to start a family, and this happens to be the best time for them to do so. We cannot look at women who are pregnant as an impediment to their involvement with us. Instead, we can choose to use the time that we do have with them wisely because they still have a great deal to offer regardless of their pregnancy status.

1. Have you or someone you know been discriminated against because of their pregnancy status? What was it that occurred?

2. Have you yourself been the discriminator?

____

____

____

____

____

3. What have you learned through either of these situations? What can you
    do to be a change agent for others in similar circumstances?

____

____

____

____

____

____

25

HONOR THY CHILDREN

*"As you grow older, you will discover that you have two hands,
one for helping yourself, the other for helping others."*
— Audrey Hepburn

We owe so much to our children who move along with us for the endless sacrifices they make. Also, for the sacrifices, all children endure whether they realize it or not, for having working mothers. But it is vital to consider that it is not only what we might owe our children but also what we owe ourselves that will make lasting impressions on them. Honoring ourselves will teach our children how to do that for themselves. In return, our children's kindness, willingness, perseverance, and bravery will inspire us. Just like the struggles and heartaches we are faced with, our children face them, too. They are additionally challenged with the task of learning life skills for the very first time. We need to be able to tap into our courage and lend it to our children simultaneously. There are countless instances where I have been able to bear witness to the courage of my children and am continuously inspired each time I reflect on those moments.

Even with my daughters at the young ages of seven and five, I have been in awe at the courage that peeks out from time-to-time. One incident that comes to mind was an end-of-season pool party for the soccer league at our local YMCA. Of course, when going to the pool as a child, there is a status symbol that they all want and look for in each other. This status symbol is the coveted swim necklace which symbolizes one's ability to pass a swim test which then affords them the acquired freedom to go down the slide in the deep end alone. Without this necklace, you are stuck on the sidelines or in the "baby" pool. Now Amelia, at seven years of age, earned this blue necklace the previous summer but, for that day's event, the YMCA took special precautions. They had asked that all children re-test to earn an orange necklace to wear for that day. What? Okay, no biggie, right? Just take another test.

After about an hour of waiting in line it was now my daughters' turn to prove their abilities in this one lap swim test, thirty seconds of treading water, and then demonstrate the ability to climb out of the pool with no assistance. My five-year-old Julianne was called to go first. She had not swum in almost a year and had never mastered swimming a lap without assistance. I, of course, was not going to remind her of this. I loved that she dared to try to do the test. She started with dog paddling which is not an approved stroke for this test and was asked to come back another time. Ouch, that hurt my heart, and hers, too. Tears started to roll down Julianne's face and she buried her face into her cupped hands. I hugged her for comfort and acknowledged her bravery.

The two of us waited on the side of the pool while Amelia took her chance at earning the necklace. Amelia completed the one lap with little issue. But while treading water, she had a look of fear wash over her face. The lifeguard talked with her while this was happening to see if she could ease her fear. With no luck, the lifeguard asked her to come to the side of the pool and pull herself out. The lifeguard explained that she needed Amelia to be able to complete the test without being afraid so that she knew she was both capable and comfortable completing the tasks. I most definitely saw what the lifeguard saw and agreed with the assessment. It still hurt. Amelia was visibly sad fighting back tears. She walked over to me and asked, "When can I test again?" Oh, that's my brave girl! I told her how proud I was of her and shared that sometimes we lose our strength and get afraid at times when we are out of practice, but that she could try the test every time we came back to the pool if she wanted. Even at that moment when her fear was raw, she was ready to face it again. That was pure inspiration.

Reflection: One way in which I have learned to honor myself more as I have gotten older is to be able to set boundaries with my time. I've been guilty of using both of my hands to help others on many occasions then running out of time and energy and not being able to help myself. The ability to step boundaries to protect my time is necessary for me to be successful in my schooling. This time returning to school is the first instance where I am employed full-time and a mom. In the beginning of the semester, I said "yes" to all things as I usually had prior to starting school. I did all household and personal tasks during waking hours then did all my school obligations while others slept. I do still complete schoolwork while others are sleeping but I ensure I also get the sleep I need where before I was not. I also now will delay certain personal tasks to work on schoolwork during the day on the weekends which helps my children to see that I must work hard for goals that I have and delay doing "fun" things until the work is done. They get exposed to the struggles I experience which is helping them to learn so that everything is not easy, and it takes practice to get better at things.

1. How have you seen specific character traits that you have shown up
   in the little ones in your life?

____

____

____

____

____

____

2. How have specific character traits you saw in them motivated you?

____

____

____

____

____

____

3. What lessons are children in your life learning through witnessing
   your actions?

____

____

____

____

____

____

26

IT IS THE LITTLE THINGS

---

*"Enjoy the little things in life, for one day you may look back
and realize they were the big things."*

— Robert Brault

There are many lessons we can learn from our children. They are young and innocent and hopefully have had few negative experiences to taint their outlook on life. They help to remind us of the things that are important. I recall a day that my youngest daughter, Julianne at the age of six, had gone to the orthodontist to get a spacer placed on the roof of her upper jaw. This is one of those times when you must remind yourself as a parent why you're doing this very thing that will bring pain to your child. This spacer was designed to help widen Julianne's upper jaw so that her teeth will eventually come in straighter and align with the teeth of her bottom jaw. During the entire procedure, she was such a champ and powered through the pain. Once the visit was complete, Julianne's dentist gave her a $5 gift card to McDonald's to get an ice cream, which she gladly accepted. We drove straight to McDonald's and she ordered a vanilla sundae with warm chocolate syrup. I enjoyed watching her happily eat her ice cream.

That same night we made banana bread with two aging bananas that we planned to take to soccer games the next day. While mixing the batter I overheard Julianne saying to herself, "This was the best day ever, I had ice cream, and I am getting to make muffins." I was in awe that my six-year-old thought this was the best day ever. She chose to focus on the highlights of her day instead of the pain she experienced at the dentist. That moment was such a great reminder of how important it is to practice gratitude by acknowledging all the things that are going right in our lives and being thankful for what we do have.

It is amazing how when we choose to highlight the positive things in our lives, our mood improves. I tend to gain more energy when I do this as well. We can use that relief and energy to carry us through unpleasant times. The downs we experience in life will always show up in some shape or form but the wins, to include the little people in our lives, will not. If we continue to wait until the time is just right to focus on those little things, that time may never come, or we will come to realize it is too late.

Reflection: I've been able to apply the re-framing my daughter did the day of her dental procedure to many aspects of my life. When I'm starving at the end of a long day's work and it starts to negatively impact my mood and affects my relationships, I stop to re-frame. I remind myself that I am grateful that I have the food I need to nourish my body, which then helps to change my mood. It then gives me the ability to have more patience with others during these uncomfortable moments. This re-framing also came handy during holiday shopping this year. My husband and I ended up going shopping together the weekend before Christmas because I had to complete work for my school semester up until that point. While shopping, I was able to reflect on the fact that this may be the second time ever that he and I have gone shopping together during our marriage because of his previous military commitments. I was better able to cherish this reality and enjoyed hearing his input for gift ideas more that I probably would have had I not shifted my thinking.

1. What are the little things in your life that make your day a little sweeter or run smoother and that give you a smile, a heart flutter, or tingles?

2. How do you give those little things adequate attention?

____

____

____

____

____

____

____

3. How have your or how can you re-frame a difficult situation to see the brighter side of things?

____

____

____

____

____

____

____

____

PART SIX

UNCOVERED LESSONS

Do you have those people in your life that are great at pointing out the positives in a negative situation the moment you share bad news? The bad news, where you did not get into the school you applied to, get hired into a dream job, or even get the promotion within the same company you have been busting your ass off for. Well, this section is going to do just that. I have not always been fortunate to have someone physically present during challenging times because of where I have been located geographically, but I have been blessed to be able to call people in those dark moments to get that extra nudge or motivation needed to not give up. Hopefully, you can learn from the lessons I discovered through those not-so-pleasant moments and use them to keep trudging along.

Reflection: There were times when family members close to me passed away and the support I received from friends helped me to get through those unbearable losses. Those times helped me to learn that connection fosters an environment for healing where isolation prevents healing. Those losses also taught me how precious life is and are a constant reminder to not take the time we have with others for granted.

1. What situations come to mind for you where you were grateful for the support you received during tumultuous times?

____

____

____

____

____

2. What lesson was gleaned through that trial?

____

____

____

____

____

27

DON'T TAKE THE FIRST "NO" AS YOUR FINAL ANSWER

"I refused to take no for an answer."

— Bessie Coleman

This lesson changed the trajectory of my life. When you know what you want to be doing with your life, stick to that, and do not give up. At a young age, I decided I wanted to be a psychologist or have a career in the counseling field. That seed of yearning was planted when a family member of mine was greatly impacted negatively due to their mental illness. I got my bachelor's degree in psychology but went into the Army immediately after graduating. I entered the communications field which put my aspirations of being a psychologist on hold. However, the desire to work in the social services and mental health field did not go away. I joke now that I was also a social worker in the Army because I provided case management services in addition to my Army duties. I loved that aspect of my military career, taking care of soldiers. Nearing the end of my military career, I stumbled upon the field of Social Work and found an in-person university where we lived in Washington, DC.

I decided that I wanted to start my classes in the fall of 2012 but was not getting out of the military until January 2013. The graduate school had a rule that no student could work full-time along with being enrolled in classes full-time. When I applied to start courses in August 2012, about six months before my service ended, the program admissions called and told me that I could not start until I got out of the military. The problem was that they only allowed new students to start in the fall. So, I would have to wait another six months after I separated from service before I could start the program. I asked to speak with the head of the program to

95

plead my case, to explain how I was getting out of the Army specifically to pursue a career in Social Work. If I waited until after separation, I would no longer be living in that area long enough to complete the degree before our next military move. All those factors made it even more important for me to start the program in the fall of 2012.

Well, my argument worked, and I was able to show the program that I could do it. I held myself accountable to manage a full-time job, and full-time schoolwork, and worked it out with my internship site supervisor at the time to do more hours during the winter break to make up for starting my hours late. At times, when a "no" stands in the way of your dreams does not make sense, challenge it. Only you know you and there are always wonderful individuals out there willing to bend the rules to support you. But you'll never know if you accept the first "no."

Reflection: I am glad I held onto this lesson mentioned above because I found myself in a similar scenario ten years later after having applied to and been accepted into the Ph.D. program for social work at this same university. I had received an email from one of my professors where they introduced themselves to those enrolled in their upcoming class. They had asked that we reply to their email with answers to specific questions as a way for them to get to know us. I was pleasantly surprised to have received the email and gladly responded to the questions. I was open and honest with the fact that I was a full-time working mom of three young children. I did not feel as if there were any reason not to share this information.

A couple days later I received an email back asking to set up a meeting to discuss whether this was the right time for me to pursue this degree due to the stage of life I found myself in, hence being a full-time working mother. I was socked to be reading the response but went forward with having the meeting to further discuss. During our meeting, I laid out the reasons why this was the right time for me to be pursuing the degree. The professor thanked me for the information shared and I moved forward with starting the program. I ended up doing well in the first semester and I did not feel as if the teacher ever mistreated me during that time, but I do wonder if this question would have been posed to a full-time working dad. Either way, I stood my ground and continued to pursue my goal.

1. What comes to mind or who comes to mind when you hear the word "no?"

---

2. Is there a "no" that you accepted in the past that wished you had not? What is stopping you from revisiting that?

28

POWER

"You've always had the power my dear, you just had to learn it for yourself."
— The Wizard of Oz

There was a time when I thought I had lost my power. I've felt this way each time I had a military move as a military spouse. Why was that? I questioned if I would fit in, if I would be good enough, and if I could find my way. When I was stationed in Hawaii in 2018, working at the non-profit organization, I thought I may have lost my power for good. You know, that real power where you are not second-guessing your decisions and don't have to double and triple-check your work for mistakes. Questioning where I went wrong and why I couldn't get something right. When we start to go down that path, we tend to get tunnel vision. I had tunnel vision at that point.

About three months into my position as a Clinical Director for that same homeless shelter previously mentioned, I kept telling myself to stick it out, that I would find my way, and to give it at least a year. Whoever gave me the advice to wait at least a year was wrong. Do not stay in a position where you are not happy. But in that position, the more I tried, and the harder and longer I worked, I saw no change.

As a woman, you must be able to recognize your power and your worth because there will be people that do not want to acknowledge that you've got it. They want to block your power because of either intimidation or their struggles that blind them to see the positives that could come from you. Once you realize that your worth and power are not valued by employers or the organization you are in, that is when you must make the hard decision to leave.

I decided to leave that position because I could no longer recognize myself. I was miserable and my unhappiness was breaking down my family. Once I had lost my power, I did not know how to find it. Thankfully, I was surrounded by other supportive women and military spouses, near and far, and my husband who reminded me of the badass clinician I am. I applied to other job openings and eventually found myself in an organization that supported me and celebrated my achievements, which overall helped me to see my power within. I had not lost it after all, I had just lost my ability to see it.

Reflection: It is difficult to read about the person I had become in that situation mentioned above, as if I do not recognize her, but I can remember what that felt like. I find that I tend to have more power come to light when I am speaking up for others or advocating for a cause I truly believe in. Now, when I have similar feelings as if someone is trying to steal my thunder, I check myself and ask, "What would you say if this was happening to a friend or a client?" This change in perspective helps me to tap into the inner strength that is always there but not always easy to access. We are equally deserving to use our strength to stand up for ourselves just as we would for anyone.

1. Have you found yourself in a situation where you felt as if your power had been taken right out from under you? What were the warning signs that led you to this point?

____

____

____

____

____

2. If you were able to regain that power, who or what helped to bring that back? What lesson did you learn from overcoming this test?

____

____

____

____

____

29

SCAPEGOATS & SHAME

"What we don't need in the midst of struggle is shame for being human."
— Brené Brown

One thing to keep in the back of your mind is how your military spouse, nomad, or pioneer status could be used against you. But do not automatically assume this. I've always had the fear I would not be hired each time I moved because it is known military spouses will eventually leave every two to three years. While stationed in Hawaii working in that same non-profit organization, almost fifty percent of the employees employed there were military spouses. Not being locals of Hawaii, we were already different, but adding our military connection tends to separate us even more. I would like to think that we are different because we are special. We have magic to bestow on this organization that no one else does. We offer perspectives that no one else may even consider.

I recall one day sitting in a "numbers" meeting for this very same non-profit where the leadership was questioned by their headquarters about the delayed timelines of services being provided and wanted reasons for why things were getting done certain ways. One of the top leadership members said, "We have a lot of military spouses, and they don't always understand how or why things are done."

I was taken aback by this response. Was this true? Were military spouses completely responsible for the current state of the organization? There were countless times when I and other military spouses in the organization offered suggestions on how to get tasks done in more efficient manners, but those ideas were repeatedly shot down. This perpetual resistance eventually turned to shame because our status as military spouses kept being used against us. I knew having military spouses on staff was not the reason for setbacks. I was shocked to hear this being used as an excuse. What's even worse was the reasoning was accepted.

Never have shame for who you are because you are either a military spouse, veteran, or brave woman that has packed up your entire life to take on a new adventure. This ideology is not a new concept for the communities surrounded by military installations. You are valuable. These organizations need you. They are the ones who need to learn to adapt and use the skills you bring to the table. When these organizations do not give you a seat at the table, it is surely time to either make room for yourself or to find another table. If it is obvious that it is time to go, start looking for other opportunities, i.e., another table, while you are employed so you can put in your two-week notice and gracefully leave.

Reflection: Years after I left this organization I received a message over the social media platform, LinkedIn. It was from a veteran who had stayed at the homeless shelter one point in time, is no longer homeless, and is enrolled in a college program. The veteran thanked me for playing a role in their life while at the homeless shelter. It feels good to know that it did not matter to them that I am a military spouse, it mattered that I did my job. At times it can get overwhelming and demotivating to get wrapped up in the politics of an organization. When you find yourself feeling these ways, look to the mission of the organization and those you directly impact to remind you why you are there.

1. Are there times you felt as if your status as a military spouse, veteran, or "out-of-towner" were used against you? If so, how did this show up for you?

____

____

____

____

____

2. What tactics did you employ to eventually get a seat at a table that values your skills despite your status?

____

____

____

____

____

30

MY INVALID FEAR

"Great fear is concealed under daring."

— Lucan

I grew up in a place of whiteness. I grew up in upstate New York where there were white people, white snow, and a white sky from the endless dreariness and cold. I also grew up in a household where the *Fresh Prince of Bel-Air* did not play on our television, as it was not allowed. It was instilled in me and my siblings early on that we were supposed to marry people that looked like us. I question today how I would even know what this meant as a young teenager. Now I know that this only protected my siblings and I within the walls and town where we lived. It did me no good when I graduated from high school, went to college, and then off to serve in the military.

I cannot remember what I thought about my race before I graduated from high school, it was never really talked about from what I can recall. I do remember how I felt when I went to college and was surrounded by many new races, cultures, ethnicities, and religions I had never been exposed to. I felt different and I also remember not knowing how to act. I was confused because this was not something that was taught to me or explained. As an adult, I understand that we should not have to worry about acting in a certain way when being around someone different than us. We should remain curious, gain knowledge from each other about the differences, and respect alike.

When I entered the military, that silly rule about marrying people that looked like you went out the window. It blew in the breeze right out of the car window I drove myself away in as I left home. Early in 2008, I began dating another service member of mixed race, where his skin did not look like mine the slightest. When my stepfather was made aware of that relationship, he went three months without speaking to me. I opened up to the person I was dating about the situation, and he chose to stop speaking to me as well. I found myself alone, confused, and sad. I look back on it wishing we could have had a real conversation about the elephant in the room.

As a military spouse, veteran, or pioneer, you will do just as I did when I left for college, for the military, and when I PCS'd as a military spouse. You may either go by choice or be uprooted into new states and new countries where you may feel different. The language will be different, the food will be different, your accent will sound off, and most definitely, even the way you look and dress will be different. When I moved to El Paso in 2014, on the Mexican border, I was very much aware that I was different.

Simply put, I felt as if I did not belong because of the color of my skin. This was a fear very different from when I served in the military. It was almost as if the uniform I wore in the military was like a cape of some sort. It protected me from feeling out of place, my uniform was a signal for others, signaling that was why I was there. As a spouse, I did not have a uniform to silently signal why I was there. With bare white skin, I now feared that I would not be accepted in my new community. I knew this was a fear that I would need to get past to meet my personal goal of becoming a licensed clinician with my own career.

That fear did not just melt away; it was silently whispering to me when I went out into the community to go shopping or when I went to job interviews. I had to constantly remind myself that I had talents to share and that I needed to put myself out there. I did eventually get employed and was lucky enough to have wonderful coworkers that lived in the community and some military spouse coworkers. Of course, getting employed did not fully erase my fears, I was still worried about whether I would be accepted by my clients. I know now that I may never fit the expectations of what my clients have for me, and I will never be able to relate to everything my clients have gone through. But I can learn to be present to receive whatever it is they need to heal from no matter the color of my skin. This will be the same for you when you are working with your clients, customers, community partners, employees, or coworkers.

While in Hawaii, we received military orders to move to the state of Virginia. We had planned for this to be our last move and I was excited to be able to find lasting employment. I assumed I would have no issues at this point with getting employed. But wouldn't you know, I received the most discrimination from someone that looked just like me. I was not expecting to be treated better, I just did not expect to be treated less than others. *"You are not from here"* was the reason why I had not been selected for the positions I wanted. That phrase still haunts me.

Since then, I decided to take a chance on myself. I applied for a job, well many jobs, with an organization that fed my soul in the past and I had high hopes that it could continue to do so. I did not get hired for the jobs I was overqualified for, I got hired for one I was not completely qualified for. I almost did not apply for that position. When I went into the interview for it, I explained that even though I did not meet all the requirements for the position, I had a strong desire to work with the veteran population and wanted to receive all the training available to be fully qualified to serve in that role. The company ended up selecting me.

Reflecting on those experiences, I have realized that I was unconsciously telling myself that I did not belong, and through doing that, I began to believe I did not belong. It was as if I were using the evidence of not looking like everyone and clung to that. I urge you to not do that. You belong. The universe, or the military, saw it fit to move your spouse or you to the location you find yourself. So, therefore, you belong. Please remind yourself of this each time you feel as if you do not fit in or if you start to doubt yourself in struggles that you might experience in a new location.

In addition to how we are feeling, we need to take into consideration that our clients, coworkers, employees/employers, or customers may have similar feelings, fears, and worries coming into this relationship with you. They may not always say it with their words, they may say it with their body language. I've had clients throw jokes with racial stereotypes at me. It's funny because I learned most of the white race stereotypes from my clients of other races and ethnicities. One day I was eating a sandwich for lunch at my desk and one of my Hispanic, male clients said to me, "Oh, typical white person lunch," and, "I bet you use your dishwasher, too." I decided to give him a taste of his own medicine: "So I'm guessing you had tortillas for lunch?" We both laughed and this sparked a good cultural conversation between the two of us. I was able to ask him about his curiosity about me using a dishwasher and he shared that most people of Hispanic ethnicity that he knew stored their Tupperware in the dishwasher and hand washed all their dishes. Wow! Something I did not know. At a professional conference I attended for women, an African American woman shared that she never went to therapy because, "I thought it was only for white women." Another assumption that was completely out of my awareness!

In a therapy setting, some clients may choose their therapist based simply on differing races, backgrounds, or experiences. For example, one client said something to me that helped melt my fear away of not belonging in the community as a white woman. This African American woman said to me, "Thank goodness you are white, I need a therapist outside of my race and culture." That situation further helped me to learn that as a therapist, I may not be right for everyone, but I am not the one to decide who I am right for. No matter what the profession, the clients or customers will decide this simple fact. In return, we must make the decision now that we always belong no matter where we are and will keep showing up whether someone else agrees or not.

Reflection: There was a situation where I had a personal bias that could have stopped me from moving forward with my professional goals. When I completed my master's in social work, I needed to find a clinical social worker who would be willing to meet with me weekly to provide consultation on the work I was doing. The consultation would go for two years then I would be able to apply to take the clinical licensure exam. This exam is similar to required exams in other professions, such as with psychologists, lawyers, and Realtors, where passing the exam would afford me the ability to practice on my own. The personal bias I had was that I preferred to meet with a woman for that two-year period of consultation. I reached out to several woman listed as clinical supervisors but none of them were taking on new clientele.

Until one day a coworker of mine mentioned her supervisor was available to provide consultation with new social workers only her supervisor was a man. I believe I felt at the time that a woman would be a better fit for me because of our shared gender but I also reminded myself that what I needed was someone to guide me through the profession. I ended up reaching out to the male supervisor whom I've previously mentioned has parted great professional wisdom on me. I'm glad that I looked past our differences because he ended up being the exact supervisor I needed.

1. What fear has held you back in the past? How did you eventually
   overcome that?

____

____

____

____

2. If you have a fear now getting in your way, what could you accomplish
   if it did not exist?

____

____

____

____

3. What personal biases have held you back and what have you learned
   about yourself because of this?

____

____

____

____

____

31
DISAPPOINTMENT

"It is better to know and be disappointed, than to not know and always wonder."
— Oscar Wilde

Disappointment. Oh boy, this is an emotion that you will become familiar with as a military spouse, veteran, or a woman with a traveler's heart, for a plethora of reasons. One central theme that this dark ugly feeling seems to creep in for me is that I have not been able to stay in one place for more than three years. When this is the case, one can't just go visit everyone because of living across the United States or the world, which also impacts one's ability to go away for a weekend to attend a wedding or special event. When you are the one who leaves due to military orders, school, or employment, you are viewed as the root cause of the disappointment and not congratulated for the reasons you are leaving.

I was reacquainted with my good friend disappointment during our last PCS move from Hawaii to Virginia. The whole routine of telling everyone I was leaving and grieving the loss of a job I worked so hard to obtain was all too familiar. I tried to be like a robot this time around so that I could just share the news, avoid the feelings, and leave. The fact that we were still in a pandemic aided in my ability to do just that. With all the throat pain and tears welling up in my eyes, I told both of my supervisors we would be moving in a couple months following the notice. I decided with them when my last day would be with what was my "dream job." I began to accept the disappointment until I got a call the very next day from my senior supervisor asking me to stay on board working virtually with the team. "Wait, what? I don't have to leave my job?"

I was uneasy about this decision because of how the time difference would impact my family life working in Hawaii Standard Time and living on the east coast. So, I decided to put feelers out for local job opportunities in Virginia. I also kept considering the sacrifices my team had made for me, the extra work they took on, and the shuffling of our team schedule to juggle until I returned after a couple of months break to move to the east coast. I continued to work virtually for another six months and decided I needed to leave my job because of the time difference. I also missed having connections to people and it pained my heart to be on a team that I would never be connecting with in person again. My heart also missed everything I loved about Hawaii, so I believed that hanging on to this job kept me in a weird stage of grief. Leaving that job was a way for me to look forward instead of continually living a past life that no longer existed.

This was not an easy decision to make, where I felt as if I was living the dream and then one day, I had to give it all up. I had that scary, gut-wrenching feeling in the pit of my stomach, like the pain when jumping out of a plane or riding down a very large roller coaster. I have closed my eyes every time holding onto the hope for a good ending. This time, my eyes were open, but I of course could not see the outcome. I only knew the internal struggle I was experiencing. I had to hold on to my hope for a good outcome and rely on myself to make that happen.

Fighting back tears, I put in my resignation. And then it happened again. My good old friend, disappointment, returned when my boss told me he was disappointed in my decision to leave. He said he overall understood and that he would support my future endeavors. Deep down I think he and I both knew this arrangement would not work out even before I left Hawaii. I was honored to have been offered the opportunity and I am forever changed by being on that team.

We will all be faced with disappointment in some shape or form, whether it is discontent we have over a situation, in ourselves, or others. We must find a way to manage the situation and take care of ourselves emotionally to move forward. The best part about this is that we have all the lessons in us to carry forward down this new path.

Reflection: Thinking back on this time, I realize now how concerned I was about letting that team down. They had given me an intangible gift of feeling as if I belonged on the team when they offered me the opportunity to stay on virtually after I left Hawaii. I always felt as if I were an integral member of the team but truly felt that feeling of belonging in my heart at this instance. This felt like a win not only for me but for all the women who will find themselves in similar situations as mine one day, where they can move and keep the same job if they choose to do so. The key take-away here is that I did not listen to my gut instinct early on and allowed for my emotions to overpower my logical thinking. It is important to have concern over how our decisions will impact others but of even more significance to ensure that our decisions are also beneficial for ourselves.

1. How have you used disappointment in your professional or personal life as fuel to keep pushing forward?

32

KNOW YOUR WORTH

"When you start seeing your worth, you'll find it harder to stay around people who don't."

— Anonymous

It is vital to know how much your time and expertise are worth. This not only encompasses your salary but all the other expectations you have of your employer. Remember, taking on a relationship with an employer works both ways. They need to sell themselves to us just as much as we need to sell ourselves to them. The further along I go in my career the more I have learned this. As a young social worker, I was inexperienced and wanted to take any job that would accept me. I was nervous I would not get offers being new to the social work field and being new to the location we had moved to.

Finally, it was our last move, and I was no longer a "green" social worker. When I started the interview process with a state-run behavioral health organization in Virginia, I initially put my expectations out there. These preferences included the salary I wanted, the shift I wanted, and that I needed to see room for advancement within the organization. One specific person in a high position within this organization that interviewed me used my words to lure me into the job she wanted me to accept. She ended up saying exactly what I wanted to hear. Unfortunately, there was a lot more to the job than what was said.

She explained that I would be on the dayshift from 8am to 5pm, as this was in a 24-hour emergency room setting, and that I would have on-call hours one weekend per month. Additionally, she told me there would be supervisor positions available that summer that I could apply to once I had "gotten into" the organization. She was also able to get me the salary I had requested. This seemed like a great opportunity to work for the local city government, put down roots, and become a part of the surrounding community.

I very quickly learned about the unspoken parts of this position. I learned that I would not have the holidays off and that I would be on call one entire week each month, if not more, based on the needs of the organization. Being on-call in an emergency room setting could mean I would have to work an entire 24-hours straight, every day I was on call that week.

One month into this new job, I was offered a retention bonus. That sounded amazing but of course, the fine print of the contract crushed my excitement. The fine print explained that the bonus was for a two-year commitment and that if I were to get promoted within this same organization, or leave altogether, I would have to pay the bonus back. *"Wait, what?"* I asked myself. If I got promoted, I would have to pay the money back? That was an absolute showstopper. I told the leader of the organization that I needed to see a clear path for progression to take on the job and it was that same leader's name on the signature block of the contract for the bonus. The stipulations written to accept the bonus explaining I would have to pay it back if I were to get promoted was a clear message to me that the organization had me right where they wanted me.

I ended up turning down the retention bonus and explained that I did not want to be under a contract. About a week later, I had my 24-hour on-call duty for the week. Being in an emergency room setting meant that emergencies happened at night and on weekends. I was scheduled to work during the day and was prepared to respond to emergencies at alternate hours. This organization was bare bone staffed in the evenings and most staff scheduled in the nights were not licensed, which meant I had to co-evaluate the patients brought in to be seen. One day I ended up working fifteen to sixteen hours within twenty-four hours and that was when I hit a familiar wall. Red flags were all waving at me telling me this was not the company for me. I understood that organizations have needs, but I felt duped.

When I decided to put in my letter of resignation, I knew I wanted to leave on a positive note. I wanted to deliver my letter to my supervisor in person and explain my reasons for leaving. I told my direct supervisor that this position did not afford me a schedule that supported a work-life balance and that I needed to be available for my family when I was not at work. At that moment, my direct-line supervisor, the one hired *from the area,* asked me how old my kids were. I was stunned. It should not have mattered if I had children or how old they were. Everyone deserves to have a work-life balance.

Although this did not end up being the right job for me, I do not regret taking that position. I learned many lessons in a short amount of time from that specific place of employment. The experience reinforced to me how vital it is for supervisors to provide expectations for employees both on and off duty.

Overall, I gained a better understanding of the difficult and important work that behavioral health clinicians do in emergency room settings and how important it was for me and those in my career field to have time away from work to recharge. I also gained more trust and confidence in my abilities based on my capability to learn the job and perform well despite being new to the area. I know now, more than ever, that I can excel in any job position, no matter where I find myself.

Reflection: There is something about moving to a new location that impacts our confidence level. A big part about this phenomenon are the changes one faces that pushes one out of their comfort zone. It can be helpful to remind yourself each time you tried something new and over time the situation worked out alright. Our feelings in these vulnerable moments can impact the way we are thinking about a situation. To better prepare myself in the future, I've started to make a list of the difficult situations I've overcome as reminders of the value I bring with me to look back on when I forget.

1. Has there been a time when you lowered your standards to get a work position? What did you end up giving up in getting the position?

2. What was it about those situations that helped you to understand that you are worth more than what you originally sought out? How has this learned lesson empowered you moving forward?

3. What is a difficult situation that comes to mind that you overcame when you originally thought you could not?

____

____

____

____

____

____

____

33
THE DAY I FIRED A FRIEND

"So often in life, things that you regard as an impediment turn out to be great, good fortune."

— RUTH BADER GINSBURG

Firing a friend was yet another experience that occurred while I worked for the difficult and challenging non-profit organization in Hawaii. That day started off hectic as usual but took an unexpected turn when I noticed my supervisor calling me. That was when I knew something was up because she never called me. I had gone a period of four months without ever seeing her, so when she called, I knew it had to be serious. The situation involved a mid-level supervisor who worked for me and had put in a two-week notice to leave; the company decided it was going to have her leave immediately. On top of that, I was informed by my supervisor that I was going to be the one to let her go. My supervisor further explained that a Human Resources (HR) representative would be over to my office shortly to sit in with me while I carried out the action.

Right then, I had that "oh, shit" feeling in the pit of my stomach. Yes, that employee was someone I supervised under the clinical department, but it was someone I cared deeply for and still do, to this day. I knew this employee had found alternate employment, so she already had a backup plan. Still, when it comes to the work environment, I've always stuck to what was drilled into me from the military: I am not friends with my employees, everything is strictly business. But to provide some relevant background, this employee and I were hired into the company within the same month, and we were both military spouses.

The more we met for feedback, and she confided in me about the struggles she was experiencing, the more I recognized we were running into similar roadblocks at work. We started to grasp that no matter the suggestions we gave to make improvements within the organization, we would hear, "That's not how it is done around here," or, "That is not how *such and such supervisor that had been there many years* wants things done." It all boiled down to us not being *from there*. We understood that we were not hired to make decisions, we were hired to just get the job done. This did not align with either of our values and this employee had informed me that was one of the main reasons why she had decided to leave the company. So, the day I got that call, I felt as if my supervisor was using this action to test my loyalty to the company.

Either way, it was not going to be easy. After the call ended with my supervisor, I immediately ran down the hall to the employee's office. She began to chit-chat, and I told her to stop talking, there was something I needed to tell her right away. I explained to her the call I received and what I was being asked to do. She had a look of shock on her face but acknowledged she understood what was happening.

On top of it, I was told she would still get the pay for the two weeks but that the company did not need her to continue to work there. I returned to my office and sure enough shortly after, the only HR representative of that company arrived. I called my friend to come to my office and even though she knew what was going to happen, it was painful. Still, both of us maintained our composure during the meeting and then it was over.

What had I done? Did I do the right thing? Was I a bad employee for telling her beforehand? All of these questions ran through my mind, and they did for a while, even months after that day. I started to question if maybe I was the reason why that employee had chosen to leave. Was I a bad leader? Even now, considering that day's events, the feelings still come to me.

About a year and a half later, I was meeting with this friend and a couple of other military spouses. That was my military spouses' tribe in Hawaii. The funny thing was all of us worked for that same employer together. We had bonded through a shared workplace trauma and came together through our common bond of military-spouse sisterhood. We all had left that employer, went to new companies, and were all in much better places.

Over tea, with my tribe, I brought up the firing incident and the guilt I was carrying, how I continued to question whether I did the right thing. My friend told me that I needed to let that go. She reassured me that I was only doing what this company wanted me to do. At that moment, I was able to give myself permission to let it go. Today, I can proudly say that she is in my forever tribe.

Reflection: Reflecting on the firing scenario nearly five years later, I have only one regret. I wish I had dealt with the emotions of guilt for my part played in the incident and talked with my friend sooner than one-and-a-half years after the fact about how I was feeling. I do not know why I waited for so long. It was as if I were carrying those emotions along with me like heavy, old, luggage that I could not get rid of. Once I was able to verbalize the way I had been feeling and the conversation between us occurred, the weight I was holding onto drifted away. Like the quote, the negative emotions I was carrying around were an impediment. I now know that the good fortune is on the other side of addressing the source of the negative emotions. I could finally let go of them and make room for positive emotions to come in. The negative emotions additionally acted like a rift unconsciously in a way that once they were gone it strengthened the bond between my friend and me.

1. Are there situations you blame yourself for that you may have seen as a hindrance in the past or still do? What is the guilt or blame that you are holding onto?

2. Even if the situation did not turn out as planned, are you able to see the good fortune that came from the obstacle? How can you forgive yourself now?

PART SEVEN

NUTRIENTS FOR THE SOUL

Unlike the previous section that highlights the lessons learned through adversities, this segment will touch on aspects of your life that you create to protect yourself from others and yourself. I'm referring to self-care, healing, self-love, and boundaries. When we learn to incorporate these tools into our lives, we begin to understand that they are the necessary nutrients for our soul. Just as we need air and water to survive, these will be just as crucial for you to thrive.

Reflection: The older I've gotten, the more I realize how important it is to make time for exercise, for getting my hair and nails done regularly, and having time to myself to reflect on my life. When I do not make these aspects of my life a priority, I get overwhelmed, burned out, and the anger I hold towards myself for not setting these boundaries starts to get taken out on other people. I make a schedule, together with my spouse, so that we both get our workouts in and block my schedule for these other priorities I hold. When I keep myself accountable, I feel better, can think healthier thoughts, and am overall a more pleasant person to be around.

1. What aspects of your life have you established to give yourself peace and time to recharge?

____

____

____

____

____

____

2. If you have not done so yet, what needs to happen so that you can have this peace of mind for yourself?

____

____

____

____

____

____

____

34
SELF-CARE

"Self-care is not self-indulgence, it is self-preservation."
— AUDRE LORDE

Self-care is *vital.* I cannot say this enough and I've learned this through giving my all where I've given too much of myself to others, and not given enough to myself. I've suffered when stuck in this rut; my clients suffered, and so did my family. The saying, *"You can't pour from an empty cup,"* could not be truer.

My hope is for you to learn about your own personal limitations. It is imperative to have an understanding about the guidelines around what is too much for you to take on and not get stressed over. As well as what is too little to handle where you may become depressed. When one becomes depressed it can be a condition compared to stale bread. When bread is not eaten, it starts to become stale, then eventually molds. The very same thing can happen to us. We've got to keep moving and not allow ourselves to become stale. Whether it's in a career, education, challenging our minds through reading books, or exercising: find those habits or hobbies that keep you fresh.

Alas, the opposite can also occur when it comes to affording ourselves time to rest and renew. What happens when you don't *stop* moving, the opposite of going stale? Burnout. Remember that we may have a problem if others think we do, even when we fail to see that in ourselves. Make sure to listen and take a good hard look inward for it may be true. I'd like to share an example of how I did not realize I was experiencing burnout and how it took my husband to help me see that.

This example is from that same non-profit organization in Hawaii, in 2018. Now whether you have worked with a certain population or not, having served in the military I understand what it means to oversee others and what leadership looks and feels like. While I was excited to be in Hawaii and motivated about this new job opportunity, I was also nervous about working in a community with a culture foreign to me. Either way, I tried to go into this situation with an open mind and to be a team player.

The longer I worked there, the more I realized that this organization certainly over-tasked and underpaid its employees. There was no display of appreciation. Personally, I started sleeping less, put in longer hours, stopped working out, and became irritable and tired all the time. I was able to give my best self, what little that was, to my clients but was drained with nothing left for my family or myself when I got home. I used my quiet time with coffee on Saturday mornings to catch up on work notes which took me until almost noon and when I stopped, I felt guilty over not finishing all my work. I worried about all that was still left to do on Monday morning. The truth was I was never going to catch up and the more I gave of myself, the more I always discovered that more needed to be done. That was when I was knee-deep in burnout and could not see it even early on when my husband pointed it out. At work, there was no voicing that more employees were needed or that we had too much work on our plates. I would hear from those that had been there for many years that, "That's just how it is," and, "This is not a nine-to-five job."

Close to the time when I was debating exactly when to make my exit, the Chief Operating Officer (COO) of the organization asked me to have lunch with him. This was shortly after the firing of my friend incident. I had been in that job for nearly eight months and had not had a conversation with this gentleman since my interview. I had a feeling he was attempting to get a feel for whether I was planning to stay with the organization. I remember him asking me about the things I felt were going right or wrong with the way things had been running. I explained how a lot of my decisions on the clinical side of the organization were being denied by staff that fell underneath the program manager, a separate entity within the same company. The program manager and I had different roles and needed to find ways to work together so that the organization could run better as a whole. The COO agreed that the program manager and I needed to find ways to work together and not stymie each other.

The last question the COO asked me during that lunch was whether I had a problem working with women. This question caught me off guard and I wondered where that was coming from. It was interesting though because all the individuals in positions of leadership at this location were women besides him. I explained to him that no matter who my supervisor was, their sex, religion, or race, if someone was placed in charge of me, I am loyal and will carry out the mission. *Mic drop, check, please.*

I was not going to be backed into a trap and take responsibility for other leaders' limitations. He also seemed to imply, in a roundabout way, that the organization had been running smoothly before I got there and that I was the common denominator of recent issues. From what I learned through my time there, there was never a period that the organization ran smoothly. Right then, I knew it was time to leave.

It pained me to quit because I felt as if I were giving up, as if I were not good enough to do that job. I started to fear that I would not be good enough for any job in Hawaii. That's called *catastrophizing*. Don't do that. We are good enough and there is something out there for us. We must keep pushing forward to find it. Do not get stuck in a job that only sees your worth by how much more time you give them than what is expected and never offers accolades for the things you do well.

Approximately a year after I left that job, I discovered that I was okay. I was actually flourishing. What I also found out was that a coworker I worked with in that organization, much younger than I, had died since I had left. It was speculated to be a result from being overworked and exhaustion. This is why it is imperative to learn to listen to your body and to those that see you experiencing burnout. At the time, I could not see that, even though my husband certainly could and told me as such. It was as if I were a puzzle piece chipping pieces of myself off to fit into a puzzle that I did not belong to. That was something I needed to be able to learn for myself and decide, besides having someone else tell me I did not belong. Now looking back, I can take a sigh of relief and feel gratitude for my husband and friends for caring about me. They were the ones who pushed me to leave when I could not see the signs of burnout for myself.

Reflection: Many lessons come from mulling over this topic of burnout. As a leader there will be instances when you occasionally must put in extra time to get work accomplished but it should not be a reoccurring pattern because then it eventually becomes the norm. Leaders need to be able to not only teach what it means to be a leader but also to model it through action. There are things that leaders can do in an organization to hold both themselves and their employees more accountable to self-care such as not holding meetings during lunch or not having meetings later than a certain time so that people are not being held up from leaving the office on time. Additionally, a leader could refrain from sending emails after certain times during the week and not send any on the weekend. If there is a need to write emails after hours, they could be placed in the outbox with a delayed delivery to arrive during business hours. Of course, we cannot control the behaviors of other employees but if you are in a management or leadership position in your company, you do have an influence on others through your words and actions.

1. Are there times you have experienced burnout? Whether you noticed it for yourself, or others pointed it out for you, what were the warning signs that took place prior to hitting the burnout wall?

____

____

____

____

____

____

____

____

2. Knowing your warning signs, what are ways that you can prevent it from happening again?

____

____

____

____

____

____

35
LEARN TO HEAL

"HEAL so that you can hear what is being said without the filter of your wounds."
— Dr. Thema Bryant

We need to be able to carry our own baggage before we can help someone carry theirs. Whether we realize it or not, we are carrying it. It just keeps getting heavier until it's unpacked. Within the common human experience, regardless of our education, training, or life experiences, we each bear the scars of traumas that have impacted us as individuals and as a community at large. Trauma impacts us all. It changes the way we view ourselves, others, and the world. If we cannot naturally heal from our wounds, we need to get help in doing so. Your family, friends, coworkers, and clients deserve to be seen with fresh eyes and repaired hearts.

Reflection: I previously shared instances in the military where I had been berated for working hard or after an accomplishment a person in authority would find something wrong that had nothing to do with the accomplishment to dim my light in the moment. There were very few instances where I received praise following a job well done. While I wore the uniform, it felt as if there was this constant competition set up amongst my peers where no one could win, even if you gave your all it was never enough. These situations impacted me in that after leaving the military I continued to think that whatever I did was not enough. Additionally, I would question whether praise given to me from others were sincere. Through processing these experiences, the hindrance from them has come into my awareness. Following the completion of a project now, instead of pointing out more that I could have done or question the compliments, I've learned to say, "Thank you."

This pain from wounds of the past prevented me from accepting praise from others and from allowing myself to feel pride for my achievements. This incumbrance does creep back up from time to time, but I am quicker to recover.

1. Think of a painful experience that still hurts deep down. How is this pain preventing you from achieving the life you want to be living?

____

____

____

____

____

____

____

____

36

KEEP AN "I LOVE ME" BOX

"Sometimes you don't see the millions of people who accept you for what you are. All you notice is the person who doesn't."

— JODI PICOULT

You may go for a while in your career without your clients, coworkers, or employers acknowledging the impact you've had on them. Some will carry the idea that it was your job to help them. That frame of mind is correct. It is your job but as soon as they run into someone that does not work as hard as you do, they will realize what they had. Unfortunately, that is how a lot of things happen in life, that we realize the value of something or someone after it or they are gone. That is why it is very important to keep an "I Love Me" box.

In this box you will keep all the cards, pictures, and printed emails from clients, coworkers, and friends where they are pouring their heart out to you with gratitude. It can be hard for many people to say thank you and to express their love and admiration, because doing this takes vulnerability. So, when they do, hold onto that. Put it away for a rainy day when you are feeling glum or when you are feeling stuck in your career. We all know that when we get to that place, it is hard to remember our strengths. When I go back into my box of all those amazing memories, the feelings rush back to me and give me the strength I need to conquer the current hurdle before me. I am forever grateful for all those beams of inspiration that I hold in my box from those brave beings.

Reflection: I've had instances when my clients were not making progress, or they were angry at me in session which made me question whether I am a "good enough" therapist. It can be easy to go down that rabbit hole and even stay there for a while. Then I remind myself that this is not about me, and that both myself and the client can learn from even the negative emotions and interactions showing up. I also remind myself that I am not for everyone and that is okay.

1. Who is someone that you can express gratitude for because of something they have done for you in the past or are doing for you now?

____

____

____

____

____

2. What is one compliment that comes to mind now that someone has given you in any point of your life? How does it feel to recall this experience?

____

____

____

____

____

____

____

37
BOUNDARIES

"Stop asking why they keep doing it and start asking why you keep allowing it."
— ANONYMOUS

When starting out new in a career or when you just absolutely love your job, it can be difficult to set boundaries with employers. One *huge* boundary you must set, especially if you are working from home, is that line from when you start working and when you stop working each day. Yes, there are times when a crisis comes up and you cannot leave work on time. But most of the time, there will not be a crisis and you might be in a team setting where you can pass on the current task to those that are still on shift. Pass it on, that is fine. There will be more work there for you tomorrow.

If you continue to come earlier and earlier and stay later and later, you are setting a new precedent. There is no longer a boundary for you. You will begin to lose sight of when work starts and ends, which allows work to become a part of everything you are doing. You have lost the boundary between your personal life and your professional life. This is not an easy boundary to set especially because we love the work we do and the rewarding feelings we get from our work. But remember the work will *always* be there. If this is a difficult line for you to draw in the sand, learn to make it a wall. You could schedule an exercise class right when your workday ends, have a friend call you, set an alarm, or be like me: I have my husband constantly reminding me to not fall into that trap. You and those who love you will be so much happier when you create this healthy boundary.

Reflection: Setting boundaries between work and my personal life is not always easy for me to do, but I find that I am so much happier when I can. I find it easiest to break away from work when I plan a task that I want to do immediately following my workday such as to help my children with their homework, go get my nails done, or to go for a walk. The mere act of breaking away from my work to switch tasks tied to my personal life makes that a smooth mental transition to hang it up for the day.

1. What are other boundaries that you can create in addition to the boundary between your personal life and work?

\
\
\
\
\
\

2. How can you start to implement these boundaries now and who can assist you in sticking to them?

\
\
\
\
\
\
\
\

PART EIGHT

TRAITS OF A DOYENNE

According to the Oxford Dictionary, a *doyenne* "is the most respected or most experienced woman member of a group or profession." Traits of a doyenne are the traits that respected women are made of and each woman is composed of many different traits which make her the unique boss woman that she is. Sometimes, we can just look at a woman and know that she is on her game. This section will provide examples of qualities, values, and leadership traits that have shown up in difficult circumstances. You may be faced with similar situations in your own career.

Reflection: The qualities that I admire in other women that I deeply respect are those of women that live their words, who set the example, who do what they tell others to do, and who do not give up when things get hard.

1. Who are those *doyenne* women in your life that come to mind? What is it about them that you respect?

____

____

____

____

____

____

2. How do these traits show up in you?

____

____

____

____

____

____

38
THE SWEEPER

"The way you communicate in challenging times dictates whether your organization thrives or barely survives."

— MICHELLE MAZUR

"The Sweeper" is a term I have coined for myself. I find it interesting that my fellow military spouse tribe friends and I can all relate to this term I have created. Just as you would use a broom to sweep up a mess created or left behind, oftentimes when we are hired into a new position, we are asked to, "sweep up the mess." Now, when I mean *sweeping up the mess* in a work environment, I am not referring to rubbish left behind. I am referencing the human resource actions that are lying around incomplete. The supervisors tied to those actions usually continue to be employed at the company, they just have not gotten around to taking care of those matters that have suddenly become urgent upon your arrival.

For example, leaders who do not deliver letters of concern or corrective actions for their own employees should be ashamed of themselves. Being the professional I am, I have no problem being the bearer of bad news. The employees know very well what is happening. Our employees are not stupid; they deserve to be treated with respect and have leaders that can have tough conversations and, hopefully, not take them personally. Those conversations help employees to grow and help supervisors to become stronger leaders. If supervisors cannot deliver corrective actions for their assigned employees, trust will be broken.

Reflection: The following situation was a perfect example of being "The Sweeper."

I was asked to deliver a corrective action once for an employee for something that occurred approximately four months before I started working in that organization. No matter how much I might have wanted to say, "This is not my job," I also wanted to be the one to be able to sit with that employee in that uncomfortable moment and lend a listening ear. The employee was, of course, caught off guard by the matter and after combing through the details, there was a great deal of miscommunication that occurred on both sides of the situation. It was as if the company had been playing telephone, over email none-the-less, to communicate very important personal matters. I encourage you not to do that. Employees deserve to be heard clearly and to have the right message received. Even if you are a military spouse who does not plan to stay long term with an employer or a contracted employee with limited time in your position, be that employee or supervisor that does the right thing. I am glad that, in that specific situation, I was able to be an advocate and help get that employee back on the right track.

1. Have there been instances when you were new to an organization and were asked to take care of personnel actions that did not align with your area of responsibilities? How did you handle the situation?

\
\
\
\
\
\

2. What lesson can you take from this experience and apply to future leadership or supervisory roles to better take care of the people in your role?

\
\
\
\
\
\

39
BE WITH YOUR PEOPLE

"Example is leadership."
— Albert Schweitzer

To truly lead employees and to understand what your clients or customers are going through, you need to find a way to be with your employees. A leader should not only just be with their employees physically but must be willing to get their hands dirty, too. Never ask those that work for you to do things that you wouldn't do yourself. This applies to not only mid-level management but senior management and community donors alike.

As a donor, if you are choosing to give money to an organization, please get to know that organization. When your money is tied to an organization, that says you back that organization one hundred percent. For example, there were many things happening behind the scenes that a donor who visited that Hawaiian Homeless Shelter for veterans would not be aware of if they came there once a year for a visit from another state. For instance, the leadership of this organization set up a cushy air-conditioned office for the leadership in a separate building from where the mid-level leadership and front-line staff met with clients. This was a mirage where one might think that they treat their staff and clients well. If you think this from going to the leadership suite and not going down to where the mission happens, you have failed as a donor and a community partner.

Additionally, if you had been given a tour by leadership and saw a state-of-the-art computer room bought with the money you donated, you would be proud to see how your money had been used. What you would not be told was that the clients never used those computers. During the entire eight months I was employed there, no one used them. That room was always locked and empty. I hope this encourages you to learn more about an organization prior to committing to donating. Do things such as showing up unannounced, volunteer with the organization, talk with partnering service providers and lower-level employees, tour the living conditions of the clients, and talk with the clients. But hands down, the best way to find that your money is going to a good purpose is to talk with the clients, and not hand-selected clients, speak with ones that have not been coached for a visit by you.

As a mid-level supervisor early on in that same organization, I was very much aware of the mirage that was created for me prior to starting employment. After thirty days of being employed there, that mirage was long gone. I had to think of ways to connect with the employees who also knew that mirage never existed.

I remember giving a development class on "Appreciation in the Workplace" with the clinical staff. We discussed ways in which they like to be recognized and that through these ways, they could feel appreciated. I went back to my boss and shared what I had learned through this discussion. My boss suspiciously asked me, "How did you come up with this topic?" Deep down, I knew I chose it because I was not feeling appreciated and had wondered if the other employees felt the same. For I was their leader, too, and did not want to find myself in a place where I was not giving them recognition.

"I just picked it," I responded. She admitted, "This is not an area I am very good at, showing appreciation." Following our discussion, I noticed ways in which she was trying to implement the information shared. She held an ice cream event to say thank you, and around Christmas time a very large box of chocolates showed up in the employee break room with the phrase, *I appreciate all you do* written on the cover. As a leader, don't ever underestimate the power of a thank you. And when you express your appreciation, truly mean it. Your employees and clients alike deserve praise and recognition. It can be the fuel they need to keep pushing longer after they may want to give up.

Reflection: One of my coworkers in my current work environment went out of their way to tell my supervisor what a wonderful job I had done working with one of their family members. This caught me completely off guard. I was cc'd on an email from that coworker to my boss and I am still unaware of who the client was that they are related to. This goes to show that any of your clients could be family members of your coworkers and vice versa, any of your family members could be served by your coworkers. It felt good knowing that I had provided quality service to this client and that this coworker felt comfortable knowing their family member had received quality care. It was the icing on the cake for that coworker to share their appreciation for my work with my supervisor.

1. Can you think of a time when a supervisor or coworker went out of their way to recognize the work you had been doing? How was that appreciation expressed to you?

____

____

____

____

____

2. What was it about that expression of appreciation that made an impact on you?

____

____

____

____

____

____

____

____

40

BE WITH YOUR PEOPLE

"No one cares how much you know, until they know how much you care."
— Unknown

As a leader, you must *know* your people, you must know what makes them tick. I thought this would be common sense to all leaders. This was ingrained into me during my military service, and I assumed going into the civilian workforce it was just known. But then again, I wonder now how this is learned if one has not served in the military, police force, or in a leadership role in general? What if one never had a leader that genuinely cared about them? How would one know how to show they care when it was their turn to be out front?

I learned what I liked and did not like about leadership through the leaders in charge of me. I knew what it felt like to have a leader that cared. A leader that truly cared about the person behind the mission, not just the mission. This type of leadership pushed me to be the best I could be for that leader. I also started to identify the traits I wanted to be able to carry in me for future leadership roles I would take on. It is important to understand that one can learn from both good and bad leaders, and then take bits and pieces of the leadership traits that are admired to craft our own leadership style.

So how can one get to know their employees? Creativity is one necessary ingredient a leader needs. A leader needs to be able to make themselves vulnerable if they are in turn expecting that of their employees. As a leader, one needs to be willing to do anything they are asking of their employees. This is a simple example experienced in the mental health field that can be easily applied to other, more difficult examples. While employed at a city level mental health organization in

2021, I was asked to assist with leading staff training. I was very excited to be asked to do this because I love training and mentoring employees.

Since I was new in the organization, I thought this was also an excellent opportunity to have a candid audience and do an icebreaker. Yes, I know an icebreaker can bring up all sorts of feelings, even from just hearing that word. However, this is such a great way to learn something new about your coworkers that you might not otherwise have an opportunity to.

Nearing the end of the pandemic, the company was still in a hybrid format, some people at home and some people at work, and the training was done over video format. I asked the group to share what their go-to, emergency food and/or drink items were that they must have if they are stuck at home or sent home due to bad weather. My excitement once I introduced the activity and proposed the question quickly turned to nervousness. No one answered even when I gave the audience the opportunity to place their answers in the chat box. So, I gave my answer before everyone and added, "Come on you guys, we need to know what each other's fuel is so that we can help each other out when times get tough." My answer was hazelnut coffee. As soon as I gave my answer, others started to pop up: "ginger ale," "food," and "chips and salsa." As a leader, you can learn a lot from the answers that are shared and from how they are shared, too.

As a new employee, I was never expected to build a "statue" or solid relationship with employees from the beginning, but I knew that we must work at it. Let's use a sandcastle and statue as an analogy here. The idea of being a leader and getting your team to share is that they show a willingness to build that sandcastle with you, just as they would share information about themselves in the process of building a relationship with you. Even a "sandcastle" relationship is a win. The efforts of your employees to share show you who is willing to get dirty. Who is willing to get in the sand and with their level of sharing how much effort they are willing to put forth in making the castle together. Building sandcastles take time and effort. You must collect the tools, digging, the necessary water, and the constant reinforcement of rubbing and smoothing the sand where it starts to crack and wear. This building is so much easier with team effort, and it cannot withstand storms with only one builder. These efforts also apply to leaders. There will be times when a leader needs to be able to step in for an employee when they need training, when they get sick or tired, or even when employees leave.

Over time, that sandcastle can eventually solidify into a statue just like it takes time for a relationship to strengthen. There are many elements that could contribute to the solidification of sand into cement, such as trust, consistency, integrity, respect, loyalty, hard work, and time. For some employees, this process could happen rather quickly while others it may never happen. All employees are unique and bring their own challenges that may have an impact on their ability to trust you or the team, which in turn, can affect the way in which they build their trust in you and the team.

A couple of weeks after that icebreaker activity, I completed my individual supervision sessions with the employees I supervised. One of the employees mentioned the icebreaker activity during our discussion when I had asked for feedback from the employee about their experience with the organization. That employee mentioned that exercise, which caught me by surprise. They said the activity was something they had never experienced, that it was a great idea but that it would take time for the team to get used to it. Phew. A rather large sigh of relief came out silently in myself after that supervision session. At that moment, I realized I was still carrying the nervousness and anxiety that had occurred during that event. This was a tiny win in my book. To me, that was an employee putting themselves out there in a way telling me, "I am here to build the castle with you."

Reflection: There is no absolute correct way to be a leader just a lot of wrong ways. Sometimes you really must learn to trust your gut instinct to put yourself out there and see how an idea goes. A great deal of leadership takes vulnerability and at times being able to act on the fly. Also, one does not have to be in a position of leadership to be a leader. In my new location in Virginia, it was nearing the holidays and the organization had not planned to do any type of holiday celebrations in the workplace with the employees. It was the second week of December and I started to become very much aware of the fact that there was no holiday spirit in the organization. This made for a bleak and dismal place to show up to. One particular morning I threw out the idea to have secret Santa names drawn and to have a holiday theme week that was of course voluntary, but it would give those interested something to look forward to each day. I was pleased with the eagerness others gave to the idea and I even received private messages thanking me for throwing out the suggestions. Initially I had hesitated to do so, but asked myself, "What is the worst that could come out of it, people say no?" So, I went with my intuition and am glad I did.

1. What techniques have you found to be helpful in building trust as a new employee with your coworkers or as a supervisor?

____

____

____

____

____

____

2. How have you learned to incorporate these techniques when you have moved to a new position or place of employment?

____

____

____

____

____

____

____

PART NINE

THE LIONESS WOMAN

You may be wondering how this part is different from the last section. The last section is about working to identify the aspects you see in others and in yourself that define a respected woman in her field. This part is about claiming those attributes and truly living them. The lioness woman is an image of strength and the one who must be dominant to get things accomplished. Many times, this involves being the only woman in the room and standing up for others. It is not easy being the lioness, it takes courage. Learning to identify those aspects that make you a doyenne and applying them in your life make you a true lioness. It is the lionesses of the world that become changemakers, paving paths for those who come behind.

Reflection: In my career as a clinical social worker, I provide therapy services to trauma survivors. The therapies used now in the clinic I serve do not allow for complete healing for all who participate in them. Not all therapy formats are meant for everyone because each person needs a different technique to aid in the healing process. The talk-therapy I currently use works more to help someone heal their mind, but we know from research that trauma impacts the mind and body. I believe it's on the therapist to find techniques that are best for each individual client, since they are coming to us for help. If our clients knew what they needed to heal, they would have done that already. I am working hard through my clinical practice and through obtaining higher education to do research on incorporating more than one therapy technique together to ensure one can heal both their heart and mind simultaneously. I am the first one in my organization to start using sand tray therapy, which uses images to process what one is struggling with, to heal. I am nervous about being the first, but someone must start first, right?

1. How are you making your own path?

____

____

____

____

____

____

2. How are you working to pave a path for those that come behind you?

____

____

____

____

____

____

____

41

BEING YOUR OWN BOSS

"Attempt the impossible in order to improve your work."
— BETTE DAVIS

While going through graduate school, I would hear the words "private practice" and would associate that with being your own boss. This can also apply to one having their own salon, baking business, or law firm. Well, who doesn't want to be their own boss? You can make your own hours and make all the decisions. This sounded grand, but it also felt scary. All the questions that began to fill my mind became overwhelming. What would my hours be? What would my income be? The decisions that needed to be made began to feel endless. But you can put procedures in place to make these decisions, in the beginning, to start to mold what works best for you and your lifestyle. Maybe you will only work mornings or evenings or only three days a week. Recognize that you are your own boss.

I highly recommend in the beginning that you consider hiring or contracting out specialists when it comes to taxes, insurance billing, and social media, if that is an area where you need to build expertise. If you decide to contract out work, it is important to review all they do because those individuals will be working in your name. No one will care more about your work and your business than you do. I ended up firing my first medical biller because her employees could not keep me straight from the other therapists that employed them. One day I noticed my National Provider Identifier (NPI) had been listed wrong on an official document. If you do not know how important an NPI is, think of it as your social security number. *Everything* you do in your work is tied to that number, including how you get paid. You would think that this would be a mistake that would not happen.

Here are a few questions that come to mind of what I asked myself when I decided to open my own business. Is it easy? No. Can it be worth it? Yes. Is it scary? Yes. Can I do this? Yes. Remember other people with the same credentials as you do this all the time. Will it be a lot of work? Yes. You are the sole person responsible for ensuring the lights turn on for your business and that the bills get paid. Under the title owner, you become the "Jill" of all trades. Being the boss, you make all the easy decisions and the difficult ones. Hanging that name tag on the door of my very own private practice in 2017 felt so good, I cried happy tears. They were the, *"I did it and I'm doing it,"* happy tears.

The decision to start a private practice or business or to have one on the side of your main job is a big decision. It is a decision that no one can make for you. If this is something you really want, make a list of all your fears and all the pros and cons. On your pros and cons list you may see things like the possibility to make money and the possibility to make no money. Think of all the times you thought you couldn't but did. This is easier said than done but you can start this with yourself and then share it with a close confidant or even with a business coach. The sky's the limit but remember you create that limit. Set your bar high and reach for it. It is quite likely that you may feel that you are never *ready* to do this even though you have that fire of desire deep in your belly. If that is you, then do it. Taking this chance does not mean you cannot change your mind. You can even start small and, in fact, I highly recommend you do.

Private practice and owning my own business was always this thing that my college professors threw around but would never actually talk about. We students were basically told don't worry about that now, you need to focus on getting your license, which was true. It would have been nice to at least get a class on what it meant to go into private practice so that we could have understood the realities we were up against. Just like anything else in life, we may never feel ready until we give ourselves a chance.

Reflection: One step I took that helped me immensely in gaining the confidence to start my own business was to talk to a business coach. There are business coaches funded by the government, usually embedded within community colleges, that are available to anyone. Just because they are funded by the government does not take away from the value they hold. The experience is like therapy in that you discuss your vulnerabilities around starting a new business and identify the goals you want to achieve. Once I was able to put my dreams into words, the coach worked with me to develop a roadmap to that destination.

1. If you have been thinking about going out on your own in your profession, what are the steps that need to happen to turn this dream into a reality?

42

BE A SUPERWOMAN AND OWN IT

"No one is you, and that is your superpower."
— ANONYMOUS

I believe the more you start to believe you are a superwoman the more you become one. I told my daughters one day that I was Superwoman. At first, they questioned it, "Wait what? You are Superwoman?" The more I insisted on it, the more they believed it and then my actions supported that grand belief. My daughters then told their brother, "Henry, mommy is Superwoman." There are things I do every week to prepare for the week ahead that allow me to focus on tasks at hand, such as meal prep, workout planning, wardrobe prep, and schoolwork planning. Having a schedule for yourself and your family are key and ensures consistency to keep everything running smoothly. Take control of the things under your control so that you can be the Superwoman needed in all the roles of your life.

Reflection: I have not always felt like a superwoman and there are many days even now that I do not feel like that. Our superpowers are the unique aspects about us that stand out from others. These aspects of us, our superpowers, are like confidence in that there will be days that they ebb and flow. There may be instances where we engage in emotional reasoning, using our emotions as proof. For example, "I feel weak, therefore I am weak." This is not helpful. It would be more beneficial to keep a list of your special attributes and to reflect on them because they may be there even in times when you do not feel as such. You must be able to call on them when needed though, which is what makes them your superpowers.

1. What are aspects of you that make you a superwoman?
   What are your superpowers?

____

____

____

____

____

____

____

____

2. How do you give others the opportunity to see these facets of you?

____

____

____

____

____

____

____

____

____

____

43
NEW BEGINNINGS

---

*"Don't be afraid to start over. This time you're not starting
from scratch, you're starting from experience."*

— Unknown

When my husband went on a yearlong military deployment in 2017, I decided that it was a perfect time to go to therapy to have someone to talk with while my husband was gone. I had a lot of things going for me professionally. At that point in time, I had a private practice in a great location with wonderful clients. I felt established. But you know that feeling you get when everything seems perfect? That usually happens about six months before it is time to move again because you just spent two and half years getting things just right.

Well, this was that time for me. I knew as soon as my husband returned from deployment we were moving. I was feeling as if my world was about to fall out from under me. Everything I worked so hard for in my career up to that point was about to come to an end. I kept saying to my therapist that I did not want to have to start over again and that I would be starting from nothing. But then, of course, at that moment, my therapist said exactly what I needed to hear: "You're not starting from nothing; you're starting from experience." Now having gone through two PCS moves since those words were bestowed upon me, I can say she was right. It continues to be difficult to force myself to learn everything from scratch in a new place, but I do notice how my past experiences make the process a great deal easier. I am forever grateful for those words of wisdom that remain a constant reminder, and for my experience.

Reflection: Through having to move throughout my military and civilian career, I've become more aware of the importance of keeping my professional data up to date such as with my resume, licensing applications, and medical and emergency contacts. Usually if we wait till something happens where we need these items and they are not complete, it is already too late. Also, when thinking of reasons why we would need a resume or a licensure application, we could miss out on opportunities because we do not have all the documents together. It is best to keep these items updated as you go, and this ability to stay on top of these matters will pay off when you least expect it.

1. What is most helpful for you when you get to this exact moment in your career and it's close to time for you to leave?

____

____

____

____

____

____

2. How have you used your experience to your advantage in new locations?

____

____

____

____

____

____

44
MAKE YOUR OWN TIMELINE

"Traveler, there is no path, the path must be forged as you walk."
— Antonio Machado

You must learn to make your own timeline. No one is or can manage your career better than you. Also, no one is going to tell you everything that needs to get done to progress in your career either. Believe it or not, there are a lot of companies out there that do not want you to progress. They want you to be right where you are. They need you where you are which is why they hired you there. Why would they want you to leave?

To get to where you want to be, you must know exactly what is needed to get that degree completed or that clinical licensure, or that specialized certification. If you catch yourself saying that your professors did not tell you the steps to take or your supervisor is not meeting with you to provide feedback, stop right there. This should be that "ah-ha!" moment that they probably either do not know how to do these things themselves or they are not going to. This is your opportunity to take control of your career and research outside resources. Reach out to other clinicians or professionals in your line of work that have the experience that you are looking to obtain. Once you know what you want, it is time to find a way to get it.

Reflection: There are many instances where either my direct supervisor had a different professional degree than I did or did not have the credentials that I had the desire to achieve. These were individuals that were in positions to lead me and oversee my work but could not provide guidance on how to reach the professional goals I wanted to pursue. It was on me to look outside of my department and at times outside my organization all together to seek out individuals who had completed the professional milestones I was looking to attain. This can be difficult to do but those individuals are out there. Don't give up on you.

1. What steps do you need to take in your career to get to the next level?

____

____

____

____

____

____

____

____

____

45

GIVING BACK

"And when you get to where you're going, turn around and help her, too.
For there was a time, not long ago when she was you."

— Anonymous

If there is anything you can do to give back to your profession, I highly recommend you do it. The best ways I can think of to do so are to help those coming behind you because this is one sure way to keep your line of work going. People in their career fields who take new employees under their wings or supervise students are true angels in their profession. The insight and experience I've gained from my supervisors during graduate school and post-graduate school are priceless. Many of these individuals take on this extra work with no additional monetary gain. I would not be where I am today if I did not have those individuals provide me with their guidance and supervision.

I am at the point in my career where I have the knowledge and experience to take students under my wing, to coach, teach, and mentor them. I look forward to these opportunities for many reasons. I love to be able to see a student in the profession learn and grow. I learn more about the profession and about myself as a leader in return. My students have always been my teachers. When you take on students as a mentor, they start to become your mirror. It is as if you can see a reflection of your work in them. It is at that point that I know I have made a difference. This will in return continue to have a ripple effect on the clients they work with and the other staff and students they encounter.

In addition to taking on that extremely important task of supervising students or training fellow employees, I also recommend that you find an organization in your community where you can volunteer. This can be something you do once a week, once a month, or even once a quarter. There are countless intangible gains that come to me each time I step into this role. It is also as if the clients you volunteer with see you differently because you are showing up on your own free will. It is much different than showing up under the role of your employer because you are paid to be there. When you show up as a volunteer with your whole self, the relationship becomes unfiltered and real. The experience is priceless and the people you are volunteering for truly need what you have to offer. The experience and impact I've been able to have on others is valuable enough.

To better explain the importance of giving back to others coming up in the ranks, I remember a day I went to play tennis with my three kids. It was the four of us, so we were able to play two-on-two then split up to different courts to play one-on-one. We played several rounds. In one particular round, my son, and eldest child, was playing against my youngest daughter. He was frustrated that he was at a more advanced level than she, insisting that he wanted to play against me. He stated, "I want to play with someone more on my level." I explained to him that we are all at different playing levels and that playing with someone with less skill helps you stay humble. That is what giving back through supervising and volunteering does. It helps those with more experience in our professions to stay humble, reminding you that we were all the inexperienced one at one time and to be present for those that need us the most. I am forever grateful and indebted to those who have done that for me.

Reflection: During this last move to Virginia, I was given the opportunity to meet with a job coach in training. A student who was taking classes needed hands-on experience to gain her job coach certification. I reminded myself of when I was a student and appreciated all the clients willing to take a chance on me as a student. So, I jumped at the opportunity to be used as a tool for learning and growth.

This job coach experience was surprisingly delightful. I had faced many struggles in my employment, and it turned out that this was exactly what I needed. She helped me identify the external factors causing my frustration and insecurities, to say them out loud, and listened without judgment. It was a perfectly safe space for the both of us to learn, her to practice her skills, and me to remind myself of my strengths. This job coach helped me continue to pursue my professional goals with confidence.

1. Who has been that person in your career that gave back to you? In what ways did they help you to move forward?

____

____

____

____

____

____

____

2. How can you pass this knowledge learned on to others?

____

____

____

____

____

____

____

____

CONCLUSION: BE A CHANGEMAKER

— Mahatma Gandhi

Y ou will probably endure more uncomfortable times than not. I hate to say this, but a major reason for this statement is that you most likely were not born and raised where you find yourself. Don't give up. We need people like you working in your communities. You bring so much valuable culture and experience to the table.

While at my newest position in our final move, my coworkers were asking me what some of the differences were between living in Hawaii and Virginia. I pointed out that the water was clearer in Hawaii. This allowed me to see what was coming, unlike the dark waters of Chesapeake Bay. If you have not experienced the clear waters of Hawaii, you must! Only if our lives could be that easy and clear like those waters so that we could always see what was coming our way. But unfortunately, it is not. Also, if you think about it, how fun would that be if you always knew what was coming? The surprises and challenges we face make life much more exciting.

One goal I want to achieve as a changemaker is to work towards breaking stereotypical gender roles. This is something that can be changed in my personal life and on larger platforms when the opportunity presents itself. In my personal life, it is recognizing how this shows up in others' beliefs and actions and in me, and then working to correct the unhelpful actions and beliefs. One day I was in the garage with my eight-year-old daughter helping her to get her bicycle out to ride. In the process, the bike chain came loose from her bike. My daughter immediately said, "Oh no, let me get Daddy." I asked her to stop so that I could fix the chain. I fixed the chain and afterward saw that the wheels were turning in my daughter's mind as if she were processing the fact that, "Oh, Mommy can do this, too." I wanted my daughter to see that both men and women can fix things, not only men. That same evening, I had problems with the garbage disposal not working. I called my husband for assistance. He then asked, "Would you like me to teach you so that you know how to do this too?" We both laughed, but yes, I now know how to fix the garbage disposal all by myself.

So now, in all my awareness and with all my strengths, I must continue to move forward and create the change I wish to see. Every decision we make has the possibility of starting a ripple effect. When faced with a difficult situation, I remind myself that I must do this for myself. I must do this for all women of today; my daughters, your daughters, and those coming behind me. We must set the stage for them hoping we are the last to endure that challenge or demand. We must trust our intuition, lean on our experience, align with our values, continue to set and refine our boundaries, and live in the moment. Always remember, you bring with you all your wizardry, magic, messiness, blood, sweat, and tears with you wherever you are, right here, right now. In all your glory, *you belong.*

ACKNOWLEDGMENTS

To My Husband — Mike, thank you for being a constant love and support. You are the only man who stood up at the table on a first date with me when I had to go to the bathroom. You pay attention to the details in me. I remember you recalling the first night we met on the dance floor. You said, "Your shoes matched your dress, and your hair matched your dress." I melted at that moment I heard you say that. You are also always willing to help in any way to make both of our lives easier. Thank you for paying attention to the details, for helping me when I need it, calling me on my own bullshit, and for loving me without judgment.

Henry — Thank you for being the spark of motivation that led me on this path. I am so lucky to be your mom. You came along at the right time in my life and planted a desire in me to keep going down my path. You are kind, persistent, a whiz at trivia, a skilled soccer player (with a goal to one day play in the World Cup), and a true friend to all you meet. I love being able to both experience this and witness this in you. I also adore your desire to achieve something big.

Amelia — Thank you for your wittiness and your love. You are special. You are such a great listener; you take it all in and reflect what you hear in such a precise way which amazes me. You an incredible athlete who continues to show up and give it your all no matter who you are up against. You are also a great encourager for everyone, including me. I love that fire and determination that you carry.

Julianne — You are the youngest in our family and yet the fiercest. I love how you remind me what hand-me-downs feel like and that you are worthy of new things too. Thank you for being my continued motivation to finish this book, as you have finished two books written all on your own before I completed one. If it were not from you, I may have never made it to this point. Additionally, thank you for always reminding me when it is time to relax, I adore our "chick flicks and chips" Sundays.

Mom — Thank you for always believing in me and for "filling in the cracks" throughout my crazy journey. When I deployed to Iraq as a single commander, I did not have the spouse to do the "spouse" things. You sent all my soldiers' sunscreen, ChapStick, and motivational stickers at Easter when many of my soldiers never received a single piece of mail from their loved ones during that entire deployment. You have picked up your life and moved across the United States when my husband deployed, and I was by myself with three kids all five years old and younger. You are always willing to ask how you can help and for that I am forever grateful.

Gary & Linda — Thank you for being the best in-laws a girl can ask for. Thank you also for being willing to edit this book early on. Knowing you are both retired English teachers seemed like a scary reality but also a blessing. I was afraid of all the red marks I would see in my draft but also felt blessed knowing those red marks were written with love. Thank you for all the talks you have with us even when you have not always fully understood what we were going through. You try to learn and understand as much as you can and that means more than you will ever know.

Family — Thank you to all my family near and far for everything you could do to support our family during our military journey. Thank you for the calls, texts, Facebook messages, care packages, holiday and birthday gifts, and visits. These things were always the fuel I needed at just the right time they were received.

My Tribe — Shaunda, Celina, and Amanda, thank you. There are so many feelings that are associated with our relationship that I cannot put them into words. You have made me feel safe in some very unsure times. You get me without having to say words. You are all beyond amazing in your own unique ways. I am here for you, for anything, no matter what.

Tami — *Blackwidow6* here to *Huskeymom6*. You get your very own call sign because you have fully embraced, understood, supported, listened, cried with, and laughed during many unbearable times. And during some amazing times, too. I will ride in a jeep with the top down in North Shore Hawaii while eating cake from Ted's Bakery any day with you, even in the pouring rain. "Thanking you for everything," will never fully capture how much your relationship means to me.

Ryan — I cherish the 30+ years of friendship that began when we were both ten years old. I experienced many firsts with you. You've been my first partner with karaoke, bowling, camping, snowmobiling, water skiing, and snow skiing. I always think of you when Madonna's song Material Girl comes on. You've been there for me through the peaks and valleys, to include being my maid of honor. Thank you for being the constant rhythm of my song and reminding me of my beat when I go astray.

My Friends — To all my friends outside of the military culture, thank you for always listening and trying to understand military life and lingo. Thank you for not giving up on our relationship and for being there even when I had gone radio silence during times of transition. I appreciate this immensely. To my military spouse friends, I hear you, I see you, and I feel you. Thank you for being the sounding boards, the supporters, and the advocates you have been for me; I hope that I can be the same to you.

Military Comrades, Leaders, and Battle Buddies — Thank you to all those who I have served with in uniform: soldiers, leaders, and battle buddies alike. You were my family away from home and continue to be my family even after service. I was mentored, shaped, cared for, and pushed beyond my limits into who I am today. I want to continue sharing all the lessons I learned from our experiences together to make others' lives at least a little bit smoother.

To My Clients and Students — Thank you to all the clients and students that entrusted your lives into my care. I know this takes a great deal of courage to put yourself out there and to lean into your own stories. You are brave to face the unknown with the hope to come out either a better clinician or person on the other side. I truly enjoy the opportunity I have in my role with you and continue to learn from each client and student I have had the privilege to work with. Thank you for sharing your stories as they are stitched into the fabric of my being and have made me a better clinician.

Tactical 16 Publishing — Thank you for allowing me to share my story. I could not have accomplished this monumental effort without your team. I greatly appreciate being able to work with professionals who truly understand the language used by those who have served. It has been an honor and a privilege to work with your company.

ABOUT THE AUTHOR

Ruth "Anne" Kramer is a mom, friend, daughter, sister, retired military spouse, and veteran. She advocates for women, military spouses, and all veterans. Anne is a Licensed Clinical Social Worker (LCSW) in the mental healthcare industry. She holds additional certifications specializing in working with those affected by addiction and trauma and utilizing sand tray therapy.

Anne received her Master of Social Work (MSW) with a medical specialization from the Catholic University of America of Washington, D.C. in 2014, following her eight years of service as a Signal Corps Officer in the United States Army.

During her time in the military, Anne served as a company commander while deployed to Iraq with a follow-on assignment as an aide-de-camp to a two-star general. Military life as a soldier and military spouse has brought her to live in Georgia, Korea, North Carolina, Iraq, Maryland, Texas, Hawaii, and Virginia.

Anne currently serves as a therapist in Trauma Recovery Services with the Department of Veterans Affairs at the Hampton VAMC, Portsmouth CBOC. She also volunteers with the American Red Cross as a Reconnection Workshop Facilitator.

In her spare time, she loves to work out, run, read, play games and sports, watch chick flicks, and is an avid podcast junkie. Anne lives with her husband and three children in Chesapeake, Virginia.

ABOUT THE PUBLISHER

Tactical 16 Publishing is an unconventional publisher that understands the therapeutic value inherent in writing. We help veterans, first responders, and their families and friends to tell their stories using their words.

We are on a mission to capture the history of America's heroes: stories about sacrifices during chaos, humor amid tragedy, and victories learned from experiences not readily recreated—real stories from real people.

Tactical 16 has published books in leadership, business, fiction, and children's genres. We produce all types of works, from self-help to memoirs that preserve unique stories not yet told.

You don't have to be a polished author to join our ranks. If you can write with passion and be unapologetic, we want to talk. Go to Tactical16.com to contact us and to learn more.

All of Tactical 16's books are available on our online bookstore, T16Books.com. Visit it today to see more books from our selection of authors and to find a new adventure to read!

www.ingramcontent.com/pod-product-compliance
Lightning Source LLC
Chambersburg PA
CBHW071416150726
48000CB00001B/359